ONE STOCK ONE STRATEGY

By

Pradip Nakum

Table Of Contents

DISCLAIMER

This book contains a unique and unusually excellent trading strategy. It introduces strategies to deal with the complexities of the market and understand intraday and periodic fluctuations. It is an attempt not only to understand market issues, but to explain and respond to them. The purpose of this book is to provide not only a strategy for trading in the market, but also a way by which you can compete with the market experts.

The trading strategies and techniques described here are based on research and development, and are updated with market developments. But venturing out to invest in the market is also a risky endeavour in itself, and hence make sure to consult your financial analysis and financial advisor before doing it.

The authors and publishers of this book will not be held responsible for any profit or loss incurred in the market, and will also not be held responsible for any possible errors or inaccuracies in relation to the information available in this book.

We proceed with caution before using our own special strategies or plans for investing in the market. Investing can be an exciting and exciting thing to do, but consider your financial circumstances before doing it. Understand all the risks of investing in the market and make sure your investment decision aligns with your financial goals and resources before committing.

If you think this is strange or a little difficult to understand, then read it again. And yes, one more thing, this strategy is not a get rich, quick scheme.

While reading this book, you may feel that some things are happening again and again. Oh, because this matter is very important.

If you have zero knowledge about stock market, then this book is not for you, but you want to learn it, then here are some topics which you should know before reading this book. I am writing its names so that it becomes easier for you to understand.

1.   Introduction to Stock Market
2.   Basics of Investing
3.   Understanding Stocks and Shares
4.   Stock Market Exchanges
5.   Technical Analysis
6.   Types of Investment Strategies
7.   Market Trends and Indicators

In this I have used the same indicators which are derived from price. The price is made only after some calculations.

After reading this book, it will definitely become clear to you that you can work like this in the market. Or how it works. Some conclusions can be reached by combining so many things.

Publication Date: Jan 2024

The information in this book is provided for educational and informational purposes only

Sources for the material in this book have been cited where applicable. The views expressed in this book are those of the author and do not necessarily reflect the views of the publisher or any organization affiliated with the author.

For more information, contact: pradipnakum78@gmail.com

Chart Illustrations: www.tradingview.com

ISBN: 9798874037062

viii

First Edition: Jan 2024

ABOUT THE AUTHOR

Pradip Nakum is an author and trader who holds a post-graduate degree in Commerce from Veer Narmad South Gujarat University. He has five years of professional experience in trading and has a keen interest in the stock market. In his spare time, Pradip enjoys writing, swimming, and listening to music. His hobbies led him to develop a keen interest in writing, trading and teaching.

Pradip has also written a book called "Random Common Sense" along with this book to share his knowledge and experience with others.

If you have any questions or feedback about the book, Pradip can be contacted at pradipnakum78@gmail.com or blog page: pradipnakum.blogspot.com.

I am watching a movie in my room, the movie was okay when it started but as I keep watching, the movie is also becoming interesting. Just then my phone rings. I saw that it was Bhargav's phone. Bhargav Joshi is my good friend and I always call him Joshi.

Bhargav: Where is it?

Me: At home, watching a movie.

Bhargav: I am coming home today; I have two days leave. Let's meet this evening and have tea?

Me: Yes, okay.

We are sitting near a tea shop in the evening. While sipping hot tea, Bhargav asked how is your trading going?

Me: Yes, that's right. Nothing special. By the way, what are you doing?

Bhargav: Yes, it is going well.

Me: Well, you were speaking earlier. Have you made any strategy?

Bhargav: To be honest, this is our sir's strategy, but I have made a lot of changes. By change I mean that I have taken the same indicators which our heads take. But executing is completely different, the way of working is completely different and the most important thing is that this strategy works in the same stock and its rules are quite different from the rules given by our head. Because of this, this strategy becomes different from our sir's strategy. In short, we can say that this strategy is inspired by Sir's strategy.

Me: Do you have time? To execute your trade?

Bhargav: It is very simple. After taking the trade, put the target, put the stop loss, it is done.

Me: What if neither of them is a hit?

Bhargav: If the target of 65% is achieved, the same alert is sent. Once entry is taken in these short trades, there is less need to look at the charts. Why don't you try this one stock one strategy?

Me: You know I already have the setup.

Bhargav: So, what, try once. Anyway, you don't get much profit from it. There is only one stock, one has to work on the same strategy, some fixed rules have to be followed, everything from entry to exit in the trade is fixed, which you call trading plane. See, this is not like other strategies that may sound good or even look good during back testing but when we actually trade, there is confusion. This is not the same strategy, because of that we do not feel confident and we are not able to trade properly, but there is nothing like that in this strategy, whatever rules I will tell you, whatever things I will tell you will do, then someone will do it. There will be no confusion and no problem will arise. Try it once for two-four months and then you will understand everything on your own.

Me: Yes, okay. Come on, tell me.

Bhargav: See, buying and selling stocks with strategy will come to you immediately. But it will take time for you to get the right entry. Have to look at a lot of charts. You will be confused in the beginning. You will not be able to understand whether the entry shown on the chart is actually an entry or not. And so on. Because he will work after listening to half-baked talks, then he will face loss and will say that Bhargav had given the strategy, but it does not work at all. And so on.

Me: You tell me friend, you know, I don't believe in half-baked things. If I am teaching him, I will complete it in the right way.

Bhargav: Look, first of all you should know about risk management. I have made notes, you should know and understand this by tomorrow and then I will tell you tomorrow.

1.STRATEGY

Bhargav: Have you learned everything about risk management?

Me: Yes. (Which is explained in Chapter 2.)

Bhargav: Okay. First of all, know some things about this strategy. See, this one stock one strategy is a complete concept, in which you have to work with only one strategy, and the stock is also the same, which means that you have to like one stock in which this strategy works. And we have to work in the same stock with the same strategy.

In: Only one in stock?

Bhargav: Yes.

Me: But how do we know whether this strategy is working for the stock I prefer?

Bhargav: By back testing. Look, don't interrupt me by speaking to me. Listen carefully, I will tell you everything. In both strategy and stock things, I would tell you not to take tension. After liking the strategy and stock, now let me tell you how to proceed further. You have to work keeping the ten trades in mind, that is, you have put the money at risk to win in the first trade, the same risk will have to be kept for the next ten trades. This does not mean changing the RPT (discussed in the chapter on risk management) by up to ten trades.

In: What is the win rate in this strategy?

Bhargav: 50% to 60%. And there is also a possibility, there is no certainty that this much will come.

Me: What will happen with this much?

Bhargav: I am telling only what I see to be true. If you want to make money then try it once for four-six months. You will definitely become a profitable trader. Anyway, the win rate of the strategy and everything else cannot be known from ten trades. You will understand only if you do at least 100 trades.

Me: Why the same stock?

Bhargav: Only because if we work with different stocks with the same strategy, then we will not be able to work properly because then there will be no regularity. Because when the stock changes, some rules of the strategy also change. The reason is that not all strategies work for all stocks and even if they do, they are not the same. Therefore, we will work with only one stock so that regularity is maintained.

Me: But what if it starts incurring losses?

Bhargav: See, losing streak comes in every strategy, it does not mean that the strategy has stopped working. We have to manage the losing streak and move forward. (Which has been discussed further in the topic on loss in the chapter on maintain.) This is not as easy as it sounds. Although it is a difficult task, but still, we have to do it if we want to take the money home.

Me: Is this some secret strategy by which I can make money?

Bhargav: Everyone thinks that they will discover some secret strategy and make money. But the secret is not in the strategy, but in the implementation. If you are able to execute any strategy in the world well then yes, money is made. Because no matter how good the strategy is, if it is not executed properly then it is of no use and no money is made. This is why I believe that the execution of the strategy will be easier. The more you will be able to execute the strategy. Well, I believe that "if you want to make money from the strategy, you have to Make trade execution as simple as possible" I find the execution of this strategy very simple. So let me tell you about this strategy.

TRADING TOOLS AND INDICATORS

INDICATORS

First of all, know which indicators we are using and why. We will use pivot points and EMA.

Before that, know what are the types of indicators. Generally, there are two types of indicators:

1. **"Leading indicators":** which appear on the chart ahead of the price, such as pivot points that do not change with the price and remain in the same location.

2. **"Lagging indicators":** which appear after the price on the chart, such as EMAs that lag the price and show the effect of the previous price.

We will use one leading indicator (pivot point) and one lagging indicator (EMA) in this strategy. And when there is entry signal, the leading indicator pivot point will give us an accurate entry so that we can trade at the right time.

Now, although these two indicators will be available by making some settings in the chart, there may still be some people who would be more interested in knowing how these indicators work. For that you can read the details of both the indicators given below and their working description along with the formulas. If you are interested in understanding this, please read; Otherwise, you can skip it.

Pivot Point

The formula is something like this. To calculate Fibonacci levels, you can use the following formula:

1. Pivot Point (PP) = (High + Low + Close) / 3

2. Fibonacci Resistance Levels:

   - R1 = PP + 0.382 * (High - Low)

   - R2 = PP + 0.618 * (High - Low)

   - R3 = PP + (High - Low)

3. Fibonacci Support Levels:

   - S1 = PP - 0.382 * (High - Low)

   - S2 = PP - 0.618 * (High - Low)

   - S3 = PP - (High - Low)

Here, "High" is the revised highest price, "Low" is the revised lowest price, and "Close" is the revised closing price.

You can calculate Fibonacci levels very easily. This feature will be available in your trading platform. With which you can do this work easily. Actually, there are different types of pivot points but we only use Fibonacci levels and know the meaning behind them.

Fibonacci levels are a technical trading tool used in financial chart analysis to help traders estimate various support and resistance levels. These levels are a cosmetic reflection of the Fibonacci numbers, which are found all over the world with specific properties.

Now the reason why Fibonacci levels have been used here is that they are especially used to check the support and resistance levels between the highest and lowest price. These help traders navigate the price of the market, allowing them to enter and exit at the right time.

Fibonacci levels are as follows:

1. **38.2%:** This Fibonacci level is the second most important level between the high and low price.

2. **50%:** This is also an important level that represents the actual midpoint between prices.

3. **61.8%:** This level is also called the golden ratio and is also very important.

4. **23.6%, 76.4%:** These are two more update levels that are used by many traders.

These levels are determined based on high and low prices and can be used in their trading strategies so that traders can make the right decisions in different market conditions.

EMA

Exponential Moving Average is a type of evidence that gives rise to the average value of prices. The main feature of the EMA is that it gives more weight to recent prices, so that recent prices have more influence and older prices have less influence.

The latest average value of the EMA certificate is calculated using the following formula for prices:

EMA (Fresh) = [Price (Fresh) × (2 / (Period + 1))] + [EMA (Old) × (1 − (2 / (Period + 1)))]

Here, the "Fresh" price is the most recent day's price, the "Old" price is the previous day's EMA price, and the "Period" MA is the length of days for which you are extracting the EMA.

EMAs are used to guide prices from a variety of sources, such as identifying trends, finding support and resistance levels, and analysing bullish triangles.

As an example, without any specific periods, here is an example with the calculation of an EMA:

Imagine you have a daily table of stock prices and you want to calculate the EMA. You have decided to take out the EMA for the last 5 days.

Table (prices for last 5 days):

- Day 1:50

- Day 2:51

- Day 3:52

- Day 4:53

- Day 5:54

Without prior days' data, I can give you a simple example that will demonstrate the EMA calculation: If we want to calculate the 5-day EMA and do not have the previous day's EMA price, we would use the EMA of the first day. can be taken as initial EMA.

Let's calculate the EMA, where period is 5 (since we are calculating the EMA of the last 5 days' prices):

1. EMA of the first day = Price of the first day = 50

Now we continue with the calculation of EMA:

2. Today's EMA = (Today's Price × (2 / (Period + 1))) + (Previous Day's EMA × (1 - (2 / (Period + 1))))

$\quad$ = (51 × (2 / (5 + 1))) + (50 × (1 - (2 / (5 + 1))))

$\quad \approx 51.17$

3. Today's EMA = (52 × (2 / (5 + 1))) + (51.17 × (1 - (2 / (5 + 1))))

$\quad \approx 51.61$

4. Today's EMA = (53 × (2 / (5 + 1))) + (51.61 × (1 - (2 / (5 + 1))))

$\quad \approx 52.07$

5. Today's EMA = (54 × (2 / (5 + 1))) + (52.07 × (1 - (2 / (5 + 1))))

$\quad \approx 52.55$

In this way, we have calculated EMA for last 5 days prices and got the latest EMA price. In this example, we kept the initial EMA price equal to the first day's price, but in reality, the first day's EMA is taken as the initial EMA.

Bhargav: You have to make these settings on your trading chart. Although I have already told you that this strategy works only in one stock. Which is CANARA BANK in which you will have to make two types of settings.

1.Pivot Point Setting: In whose inputs, Type is Fibonacci and Pivots Timeframe is Daily and then Ok as in the chart given below.

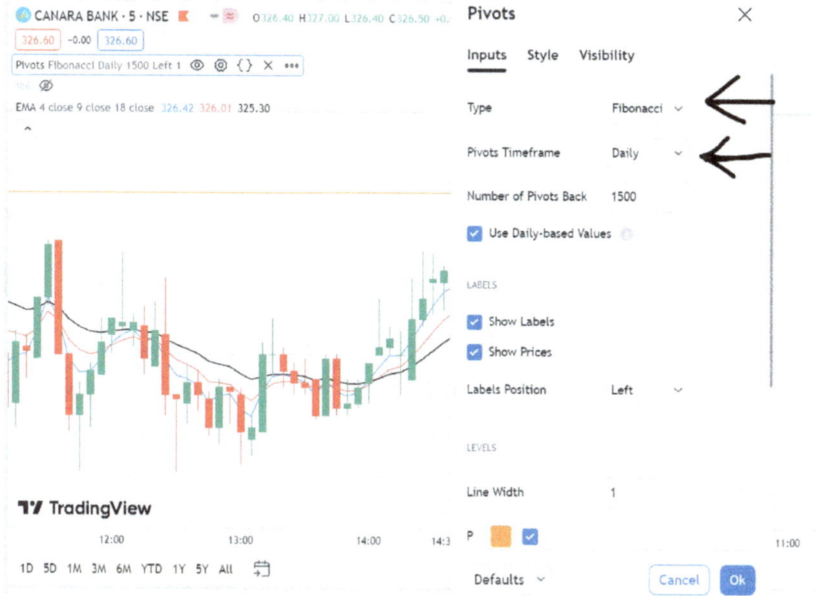

2. EMA setting: Indicators in which three EMAs come together, whose inputs are 4, 9 and 18 in length and give different colours to all three so that there is no confusion in taking entry. I have coloured 4 blue, 9 red and 18 black. To get

the colour you will have to go to Style. Then Ok as in the chart below.

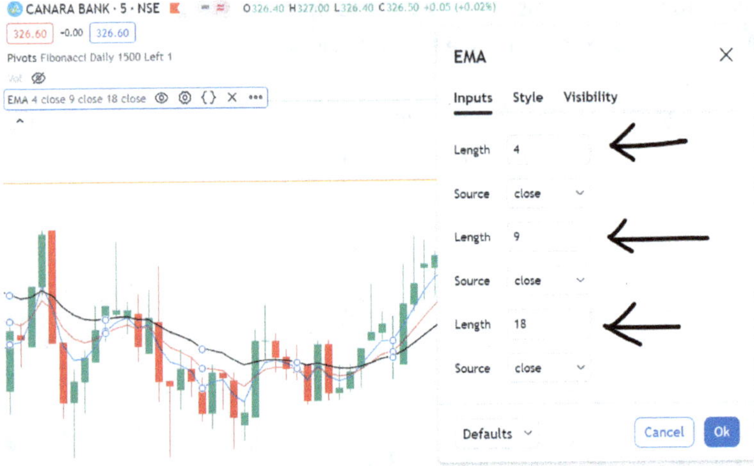

Now after making these two settings, let us understand how to take entry. For that, it is very important to first understand the work of EMA. In the chart below, 4,9 and 18 EMA is showing buy signal from 2:10. And both these settings have to be done on a time frame of 5 minutes because this strategy works only on 5 minutes time frame.

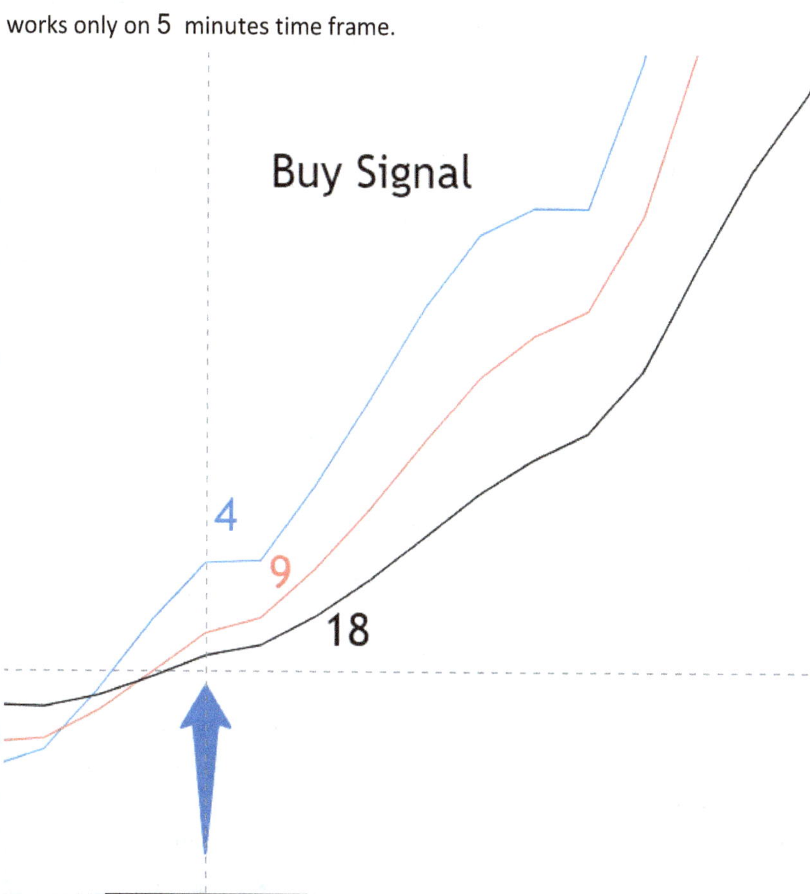

This only means that now a buy signal can come. Has not come. The sequence of these three EMAs should be in lines 4, 9 and 18 from top to bottom. That means 4,9,18 should be in sequence.

HOW TO TAKE ENTRY?

BUY ENTRY

Now entry will be available only when the pivot point is broken. In the chart below the pivot point is broken at 10:20 minutes. The closing price of this entry candle is the entry price. Now two things have to be kept in mind on this.

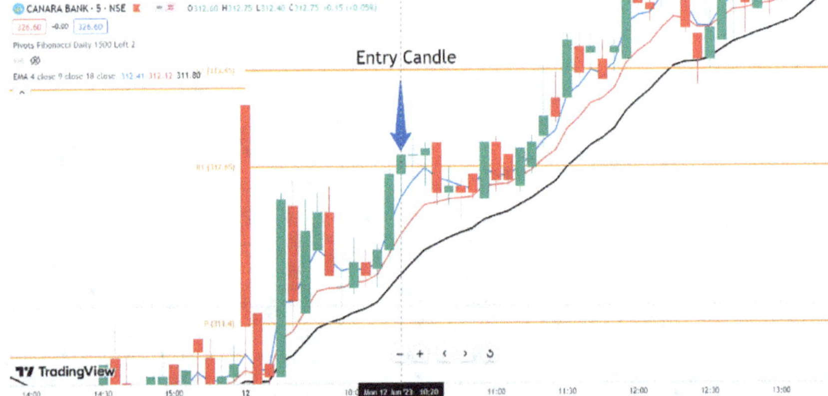

1. The previous candle of the entry candle should have a sequence of 4,9,18 EMA. If this is not a sequence then there is no entry. In the chart below, the 10:15 candle is a sequence of 4,9,18 EMA. If this sequence is not visible properly then the candle should be taken out for some time and examined.

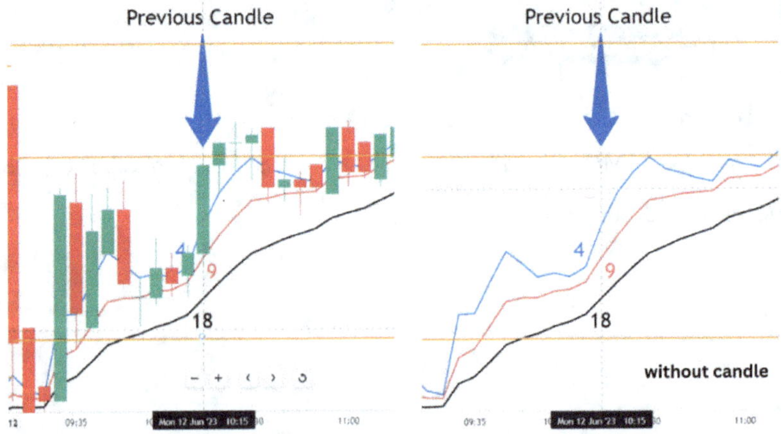

2. Which is the entry candle that has broken the pivot point. This break from the pivot point to the closing price should be at least 0.03% of the stock price. If it is less than 0.03% then the trade should not be taken.

Now after entering properly, three more tasks are left.

1. **Stop Loss:** The sequence of 4,9,18 EMA which was seen in the next candle of the entry candle. The price at which 18 EMA is the stop loss. Another thing to be noted here is that if the stop loss size is more than 1% from the entry point to 18 EMA then a stop loss of 0.80% has to be taken in that trade. In this case the stop loss is the black EMA. Which can be seen in the chart given below.

2. **Target:** Actually, the target has to be kept at 1:2 RRR. Which is placed in this position. And further let us know about all these rules in depth one by one.

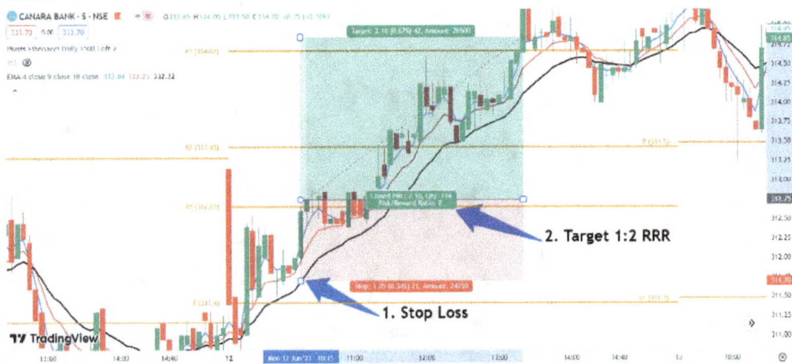

3. **Exit:** About which we will know in depth further.

SELL ENTRY

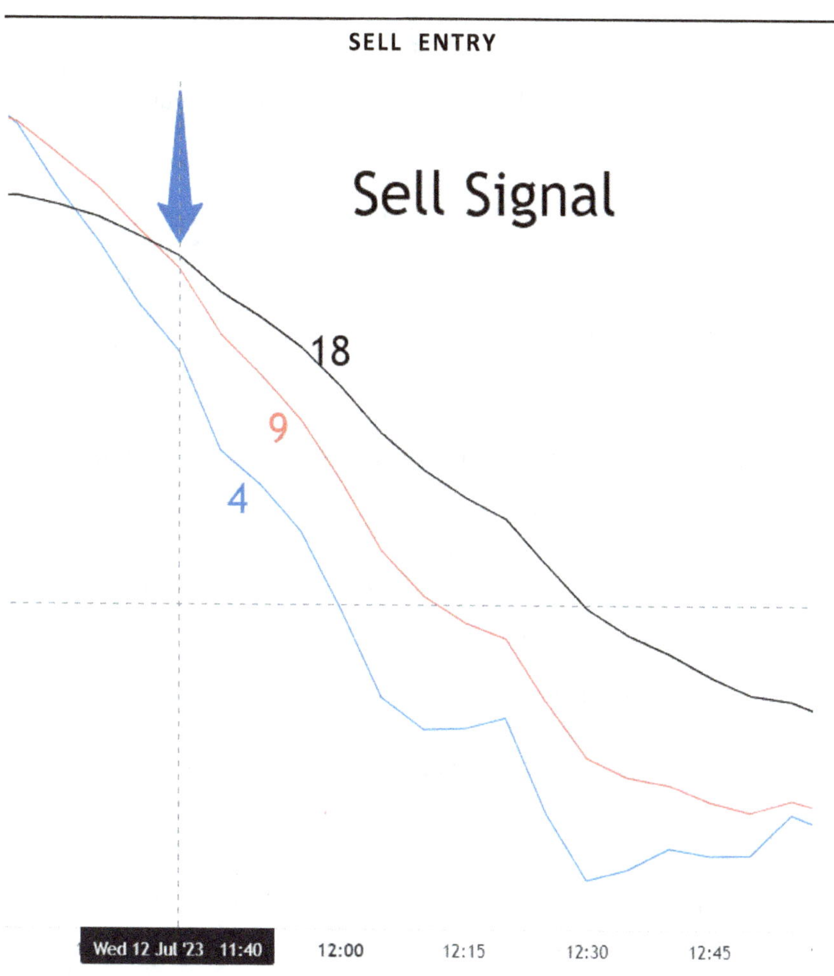

This just means that Sell signal can now come. Has not come. The sequence of these three EMAs from top to bottom should be in the 18, 9 and 4 lines. That means it should be in the sequence 18,9,4. There is no difference between buy and sell. The exact opposite of the buy example seen above is in the Sell.

TRADING RULES

As I already told, this strategy is only for Canara bank, so these rules have also been made in the same way.

1. **Time:** You can trade only from 10:00 am to 2:45 pm.

2. **When the pivot point is broken,** there should be a sequence of 4,9,18 EMA (Buy) and 18,9,4 EMA (Sell) in the previous candle of the entry candle and it should be clearly visible.

3. **Breakout condition:** The breakout from the pivot point to the closing price should be at least 0.03% of the stock price.

4. **Stop Loss:** The price at which the 18 EMA of the previous candle of the entry candle is, is the stop loss. If the stop loss size is more than 1% from the entry point to 18 EMA then a stop loss of 0.80% has to be kept.

5. **Target:** The target is to be kept as per 1:2 R. If the stop loss is 0.25% or less of the stock, a 1:5 R target is required.

6. **Reversal point:** If the stock reverses after achieving 1:1.5 R target, then 9 EMA is to be used as the exit point.

7. **Second Entry:** Second entry cannot be taken in the same candle in which there was exit in the first trade. See further details.

8. **Pivot Point Cross:** If the price has crossed more than twice before the pivot point at which the entry is being made, then the entry will not be valid.

9. **Identifying Volatility:** If the stock is all ready to move more than 3%, then it should be avoided if you find a trade on that day.

All these rules have to be understood deeply. So let us understand one by one.

1. TIME LIMIT:

You can trade only from 10:00 am to 2:45 pm. After 10:00, if the open candle of 9:55 and which will close at 10:00 is giving entry, then you should definitely take entry. It is very important to see the time under the candle. Now the candle of 9:55 is giving entry in the chart given below.

But remember that if the 9:50 candle gives entry then do not take it, do not think that what difference will it make in 5 minutes. In the chart given below, buy entry is being seen at 9:50. Which is not to be taken according to the rules.

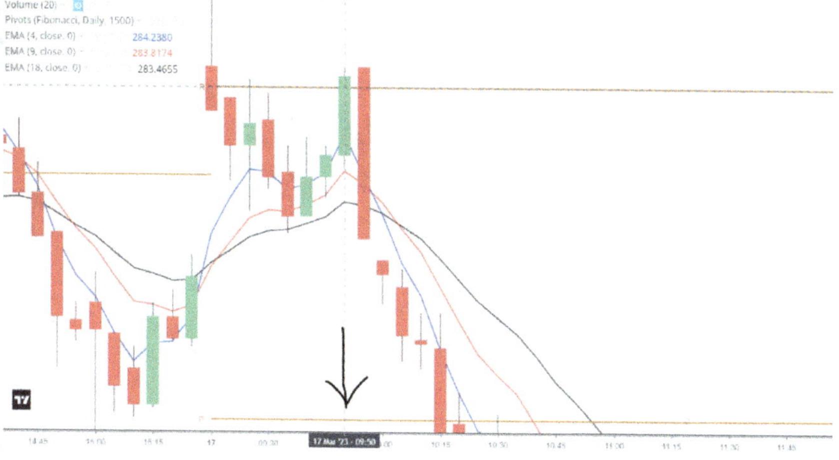

We just have to look at the candles from 9:55 to 2:45. This is the time because this strategy works well during this time. If a trade is taken at any other time, then that trade will not be considered a trade of the strategy.

Now this question might be coming in your mind that if you get entry before 9:55 and after 2:45 then why not take it, what is the reason? Look, there is a lot of volatility in the market before 9:55. By the way, the breakouts that are found are mostly fake breakouts. And after 2:45 there is no time left to complete the trade. And yes, one more thing, this trade should not be carried forward, the trade should be closed as per the strategy in intraday itself.

Now why should trade not carry forward? This is because this strategy is intraday, and it has to close the trade intraday only. If we carry forward the trade to tomorrow then this trade will not remain an intraday trade, but will become a BTST trade. Therefore, we have to follow the rules of the strategy only.

2. Pivot Point Break and Sequence:

When the pivot point is broken, the previous candle of the entry candle should have a sequence of 4,9,18 EMA (Buy) and 18,9,4 (Sell).

Now here E means Entry candle, at first glance it seems that it is Entry but if you look carefully, it is not Entry. If we look carefully at the sequence of 4,9,18, it appears something like this.

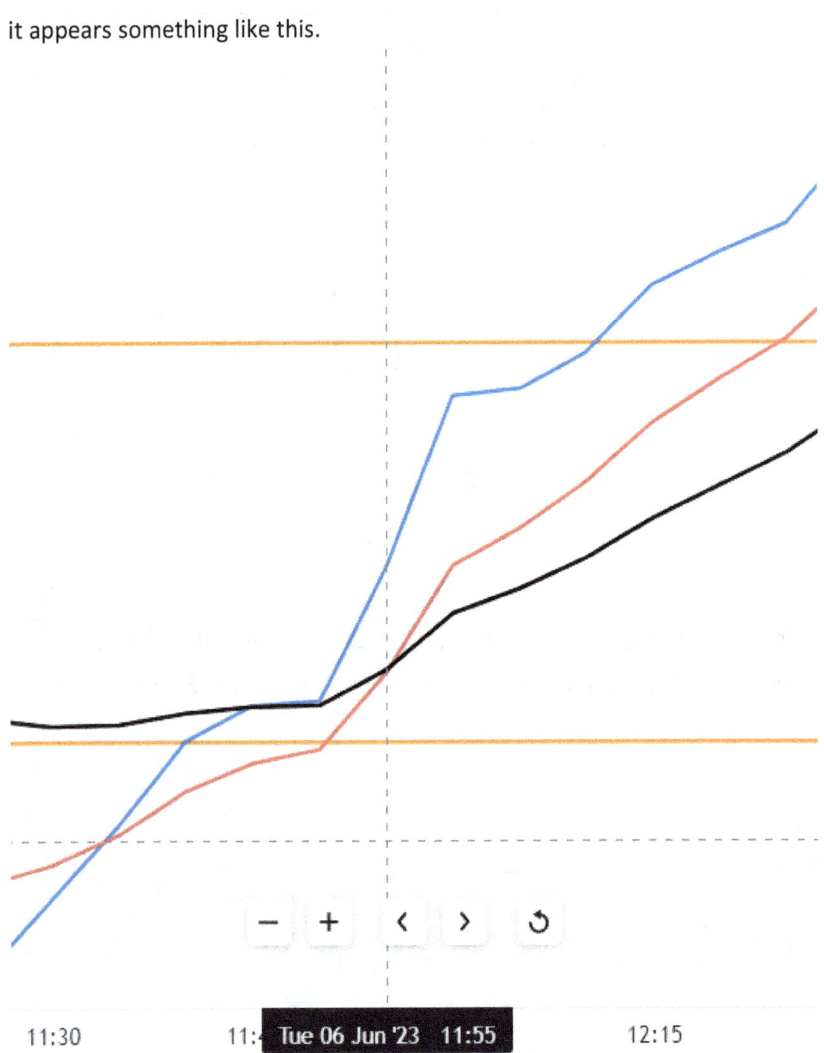

Whenever the sequence is not clearly visible, the candle should be removed for some time and rechecked. If there is no sequence then the trade should not be taken. The thing to remember here is to look at the sequence of the previous candles of the breakout candle. Two-three charts are given below.

How clearly the sequence of EMA at 10:15 minutes, the previous candle of the Entry candle, is visible. This is the 4,9,18 EMA sequence of buy.

However, stop loss has been given in this entry. But if you look at the sequence, it is clearly visible. Here you only see the sequence of one or two chart Sell. In this 18,9,4 EMA sequence will come. I know this 4,9,18 EMA sequence will be a bit difficult to remember but the colour is given so that you can remember it by colour.

The sequence is quite clearly visible in this chart also. There are only two things to remember in these rules.

I.   4,9,18 EMA from top to bottom so for Buy. And 18,9,4 EMA is for Sell.

II.   The sequence of the entry candle is to be seen in the previous candle. After taking entry on its next side, no matter what the sequence is, we have to see the sequence only in the previous candle of the entry candle. Maybe this question comes to your mind that why is it so important to see the sequence? This is because the sequence shows the price trend. It becomes easy to see the trend intraday. And there may also be a question that why only three EMAs? So, this is because these three EMAs give us better entry confirmation.

---

3. BREAKOUT CONDITION:

That break from the pivot point should be at least 0.03% of the stock price. Actually, this point is quite simple. But it can be a little difficult to use. This is because the candle is about to break the pivot point. Here I am talking about an open candle that has not yet broken the pivot point. Let us understand from the chart given below.

The entry candle closes at 12:20. If we have to take entry in this trade, we will have to be alert from 12:15. This is because as soon as there is 10 seconds left in the candle close, we want to measure if there is going to be a break of 0.03% or more from the pivot point to the price close. Then we will have to decide two prices and from that we will have to decide how many positions we want to take in the trade. And as soon as the price closes, we have to immediately enter the trade.

By price closing, I mean that if a candle is showing a break above 0.04% for 4 minutes and 50 seconds, then most likely the closing of the candle will be around 0.04%. The question arises why do we have to do all these 10 seconds in advance? Only when the candle closes can you take a major trade and enter the trade. Yes, this is true, but when the price closes, we will count how many shares to take a position and it will take at least 10 seconds to decide. A trade may be missed in this count. I said the trade may be missed, I am not saying that if you don't do this then the entry will be missed, because sometimes the stock moves immediately. And our order remains pending. And after a missed trade, a lot of mistakes can happen.

Like I said before, it can be a little difficult to use. Another thing that can make a mistake is entering the candle before closing, which is also called FOMO (fear of missing out) entry. Here the trader fears that the entry will be missed, hence he takes entry in the trade even before the candle closes above the pivot point. As happened with me in the chart given below.

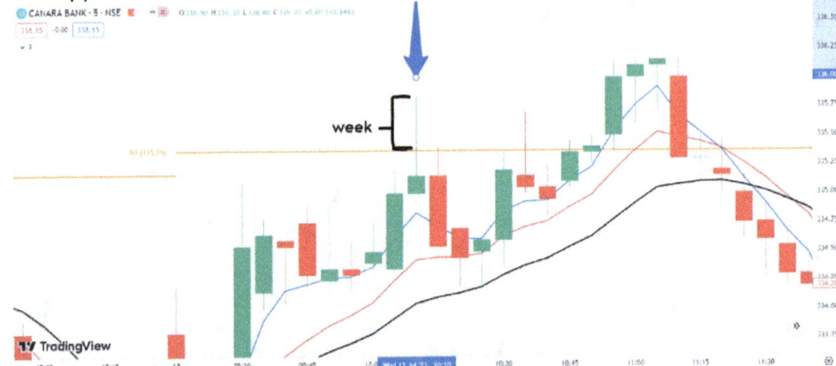

At 10:10 the stock price came very close to the pivot point, so I got alerted and the price crossed the pivot point at 10:13. The week you are seeing on the chart was not a week at that time. The candle was showing and I thought the candle would close above 0.03%. So, I did not wait for the candle closing and took entry in the trade. Then the price finally came down in two minutes and closed below the pivot point. That means there was no entry, yet I entered. There is also a desire that if I enter early, then my stop loss size will be less and I also expect a higher target.

Second and third candle entry, if the first candle does not give a break of 0.03% then we can wait for a break of 0.03% on the next two candles, then we can take entry. Entry cannot be taken from the fourth candle. The first candle in the chart below broke the pivot point, but only by 0.02%. Now according to the rules, if the second and third candles give a break of 0.03% above the pivot point, then we can take entry, but in this chart the break has happened only in the fourth candle. Therefore, sell entry could not be taken in this trade and the stock did not go down.

If the candle on the chart gave a break but it was below 0.03% and you entered the trade thinking that the next candle will give a break above 0.03%. So, you look at the chart given below, the 12:15 minute candle gave a break of 0.02% and I took the entry and the next candle did not give a break of 0.03% and I remained sitting because I am still thinking that the third candle will break. Then the 12:50 candle formed a week and hit the stop loss. And as per the strategy, the candle of 01:05 minutes gave entry and also gave further target. But I could not take it. Because I took a stop loss, I lost confidence in the strategy. Here the 0.03% rule shows its wonders, this rule protects us from fake entries.

Also see a trade with a target. In this trade, the candle of 01:10 minutes broke the pivot point, but there was a break of only 0.02%, the next candle closed 0.03% above the pivot point and the close price is the entry price and the stop loss was set. Where to put it, we will see in the next rules.

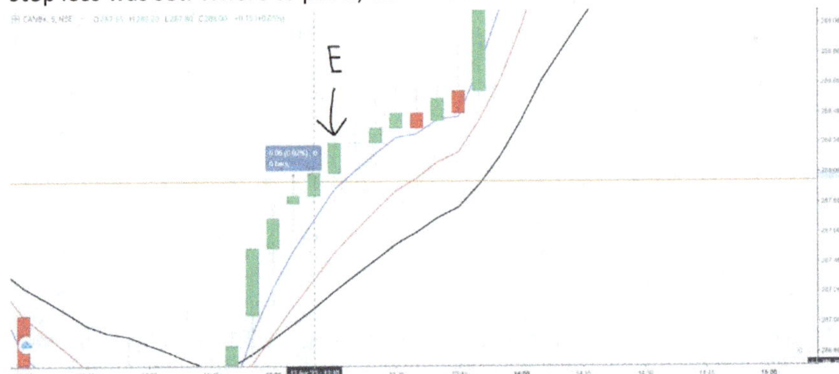

There are only three things to remember in these rules.

1. Trade can be taken only if there is a breakout of 0.03% or above from the pivot point to the price close.

2. If the first candle does not give a break of 0.03% then we can take entry if there is a break of 0.03% on the next two candles. Entry cannot be taken from the fourth candle.

3. Entry should not be taken until the candle closes after crossing the pivot point. Entry should be taken immediately as soon as the candle crosses the pivot point and closes. Till then keep preparing for the entry, like how many shares to create the position. Be prepared by placing the order in the system, as soon as you get confirmation that entry is to be taken, enter immediately.

One more thing, if for any reason you take entry late in the trade, then you cannot take entry at a price higher than the closing price or in other words, entry price. If a price is cheaper than the entry price, then you can take it but at the closing price. Cannot be taken higher than the price. Because if it is expensive than two things will happen, first the reward will reduce and the risk will also increase. Now, if the risk and reward are distorted then you will not get an edge at the end of ten trades. What I want to say is that all the rules depend on each other so much. If even one rule is broken, the overall result at the end of 10 trades will be different. Then trust in the strategy also reduces. There are many other things which we will talk about further.

4 STOP LOSS:

First of all, I want to say how dangerous it can be to work in the world of trading without a stop loss. Don't even think about this, stop loss should be set. There is no need to think anything about setting stop loss in this strategy. Whether the trade is buying side or selling side, it is very easy. Stop loss is the price at which the 18 EMA of the previous candle of the entry candle is located. In the chart below I have mentioned the stop loss size, which we will talk about further. It can also be understood in this way that 18 EMA of the sequence seen for taking entry is the stop loss.

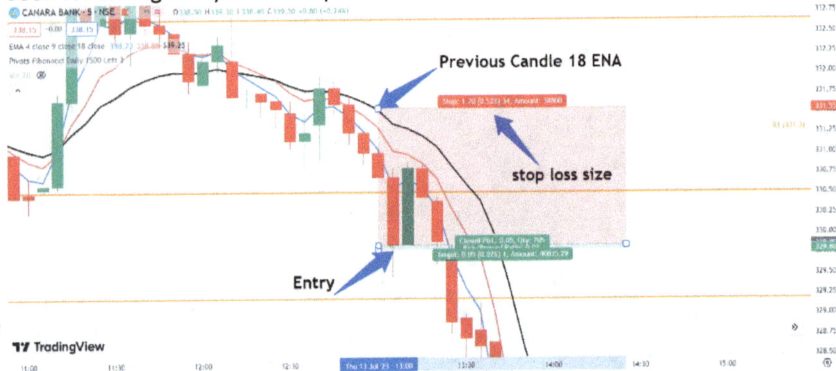

Now it may happen that the price of 18 EMA of the previous candle of the entry candle is 327.32. Now, due to the price gap of the stock, which is also called Tick Size, of 0.05, we can keep the stop loss at 327.30 or 327.35. The middle price cannot be kept at 327.32, because the stock price will go straight from 327.30 to 327.35. So anyway, we will keep the stop loss at 327.30.

Here you may feel what a difference 0.05 paise will make. But let me tell you that a stop loss of 0.05 paise can be hit and can also be saved.

How to set stop loss if there is second and third candle entry? For that we see the same trade as seen in the breakout condition rules. In this trade, entry has been made in the second candle but for the stop loss we will keep in mind only the previous candle of the first candle which was broken. Meaning, the price at which the 18 EMA of the previous candle of the candle breaking the pivot point is the stop loss.

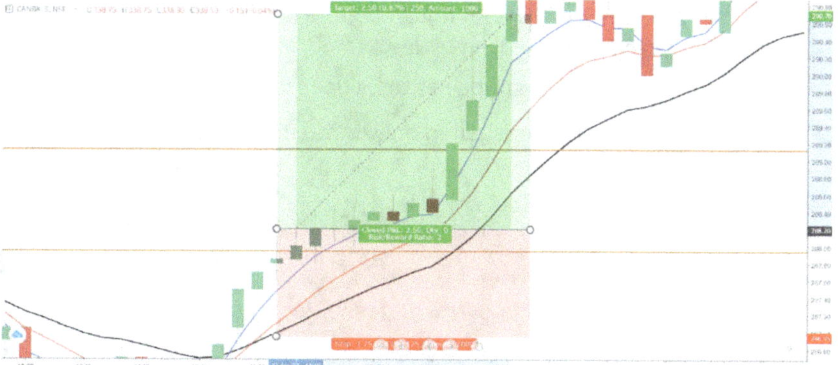

The rules to keep in mind for stop loss are:

If the stop loss size is more than 1% from the entry point to 18 EMA, then a stop loss of 0.80% has to be kept.

This does not mean that if the stop loss is 0.90% or 0.98% then it has to be set at 0.80%. This has to be done only if the stop loss size goes above 1%. Whatever stop loss is up to 1% is to be kept the same but only if the stop loss is 1% and above then only 0.80% stop loss is to be kept. And if a stop loss is hit during such a trade day, then you cannot take another entry in the trade with a stop loss of 1%.

See, three types of stop loss trades are available in this strategy.

1. **Normal trade,** whose stop loss is above 0.25% and below 1%.

2. **1% trades,** whose stop loss is 1% or above.

3. **Space trade,** whose stop loss is 0.25% or below.

1. **Normal trade, whose stop loss is above 0.25% and below 1%.** Like it is said that whatever stop loss is below 1%, the trade has to be taken with the same stop loss, although there is no need of an example in this, but to understand, let us see a trade. In the below trade, the stop loss is 0.72%, so the trade has to be done with a stop loss of 0.72% only. Changes will be required only if the stop loss is 1% or above.

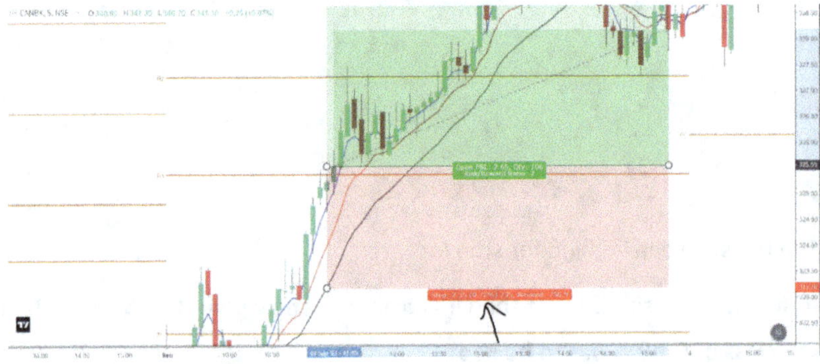

2. **1% trades, whose stop loss is 1% or above.** If there is a need to do this then we will have to see the below mentioned procedure. If we take this trade as a normal trade then the stop loss of the entry being made is 1.54%. Its risk reward ratio is very useful. To achieve the target of 1:2, the stock will have to move by 3% and then it will get

the normal target of 1:2.

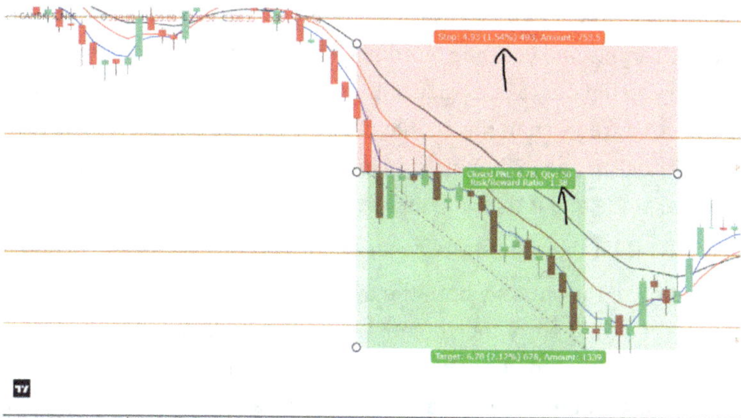

So, to overcome this problem the stop loss size will have to be reduced. Therefore, if the stop loss size at the time of taking a trade is more than 1%, then maintain the risk reward ratio by placing a stop loss of only 0.80%. Look, if we make a slight change in the trade we saw above, then to give the target of 1:2, the stock will have to move only 1.62%. If we had gone with normal stop loss then finding this target would have become very difficult.

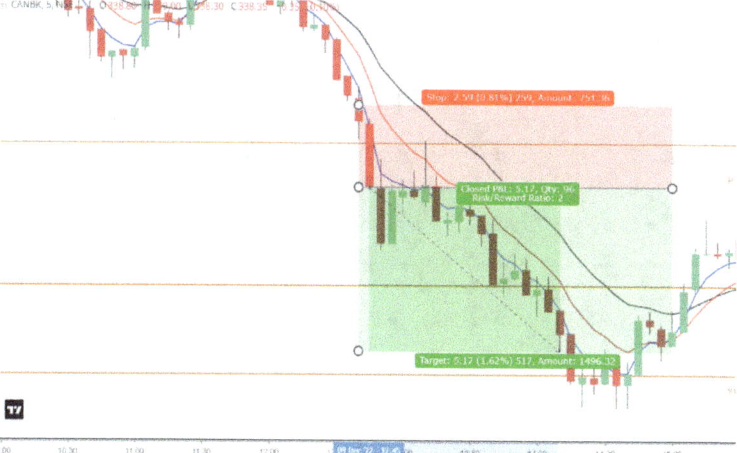

3. **Special trades with stop loss of 0.25% or below**. Because it is special, we will talk about it in the specifically targeted rules.

You can take maximum two stop losses in a day. If you get a third entry after incurring a loss in two trades then you should not do so. Even if he then gives a trade target. And yes, one more thing has to be kept in mind that if for any reason you did not take a trade with stop loss and took two times the risk in the second trade, then this should not be done. Do not think at all that as per the strategy, if I have found a stop loss then I invest the remaining money in another trade and if the target is achieved then I will get four times. And if the stop loss is hit then the strategy has already given 2 stop losses. And if according to the strategy both the trades are taken and the stop loss is hit, then if you get a third entry then do not take the trade because there is a high possibility of the stop loss being hit in that too. This is because this strategy, called Rangebound, which is also called sideways, works less in the market, so taking three trades in a single day does not make any sense. And if you have taken two stop losses in a day then there are more chances that the stock will be sideways that day. And in such a market there is no other way to avoid stop loss for this strategy. In the chart given below, even after two stop losses are hit, another entry is made in which also no target is visible.

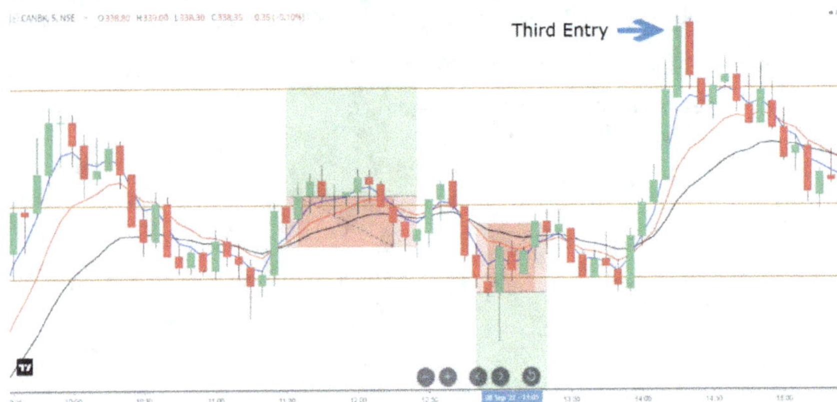

---

5. TARGET:

RRR (Risk Reward Ratio) of 1:2 has to be maintained, which has to be installed in the system itself. And when the stop loss is 0.25% of the stock or below then its rules are given separately. Like I said earlier, everything is already decided in this strategy. So, the target is also fixed at 1:2. After taking entry in the trade, the target has to be entered in the system itself. This is so that the target given by the strategy is not missed and secondly, if we are not sitting in front of the screen and are doing any work, then we can take the target only when the trade gives the target.

I did not enter the target system in the trade given below.

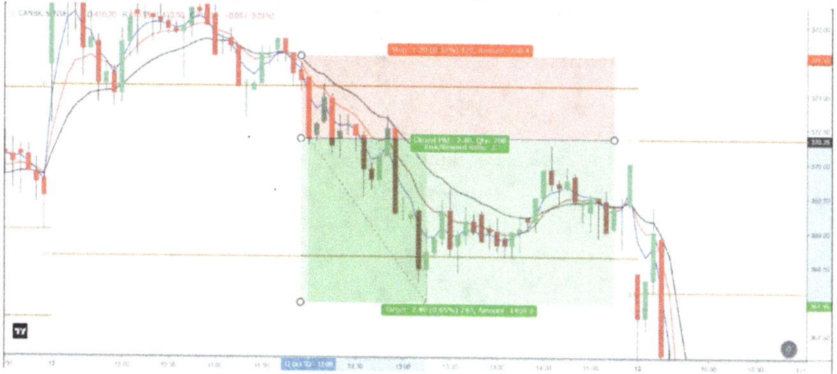

So, the stock came right up to 1:2 R and went back into the mood after making a week and I did not come out of the trade and missed the target of 1:2.

However, then I closed above 9 EMA and then came out of the trade but the target was very low. But if I had entered the target in the system itself, my target would have been achieved as soon as the price target was touched. Even if the stock just makes a week and touches it.

Now we are talking about 1:2 target, but what if the stock goes up to 1:2 target? Then what we have to do is written in Rules Number 6. For now, let us talk about these rules. System target is not set when stop loss and stock size is 0.25% or below. This stock is such that sometimes it moves more than 1-

1.5%. Because we do not know when such a move will be made and no one knows, so these rules have been made to make such a move.

In trades with 0.25% stop loss, the breakeven rules will no longer apply once 1.3R is hit. In such a trade, the fix is to set a target of 5R in the system and leave the screen alone. After crossing 3 R, you can exit at 9 EMA but only after crossing 3 R. If the stop loss is hit then so be it but do not exit the trade until the 9 EMA is closed. And no, stop loss has to be kept at breakeven. This is because such trades are not found frequently and that is why I say "if there is a chance to make money then make it other ways chance is will make you". This line is best for trades with stop loss less than 0.25%. Is. Two tracks can be seen on this also.

However, managing such a trade is a very difficult task. I am calling it difficult because the stock moves very fast and the size of the candles is also 0.20%, 0.30%, 0.60% or more, so in a single candle, the target is 1:2 or above. But it will be visible but we have to wait that it goes till 1:5, even if it does not go then the risk is very less in front of the reward, so we can give one stop loss and sometimes we have to give two as well like in the chart given below. It's Happened.

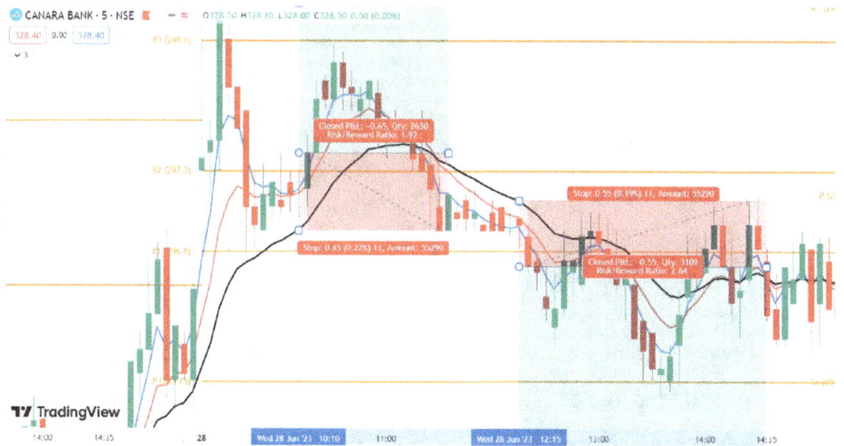

---

6. EXIT POINT AND REVERSAL POINT:

After taking the trade, if the stock reverses after getting 1:1.5 RRR target, then 9EMA has to be exited. Look, there are three possibilities here according to the trade taken from this strategy. either stock price

1. Will give a target of 1:2 RRR.

2. Will give stop loss.

3. The stock can remain anywhere in between these two.

    1) If the stock goes up to 1:1.3RRR.

    2) If the stock goes up to 1:1.5RRR.

    3) Time Exit

The first two would be possibilities. Then there is nothing to be done because the target and stop loss of 1:2 RRR is set in the system itself. But the stock can remain anywhere in between these two. What we do then depends on the possibilities.

1. **If the stock goes to 1:1.3 RRR and reverses from there,** then we have to come out in no profit, no loss. After getting 65% target, we have to place the stop loss at the entry point, so that we do not suffer loss in a trade which has given 65% target. As soon as the target of 1.3 R is given, immediately stop loss has to be placed at break even. Like I said above, stop loss has to be placed at breakeven only after 1.3 R is hit. Certainly not before that. In the chart below it goes to 1.24 R, then comes to the entry point, and then crosses 1.3 R, but does not fall below that.

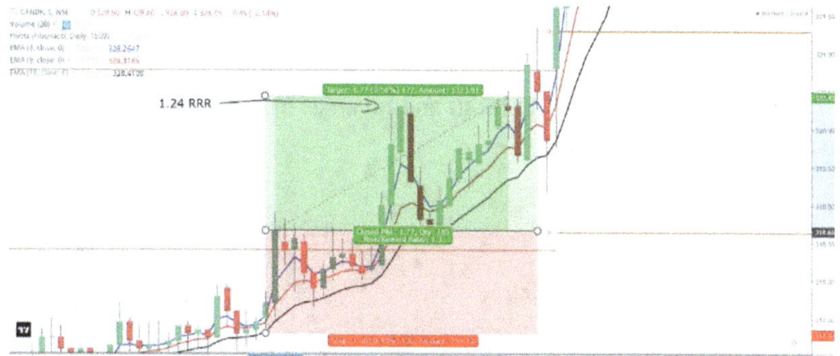

If we had changed the stop loss to the entry point after achieving half the target, we would have come out of this trade and would not have been able to gain anything from this trade. The reason behind keeping such rules is that this strategy works only if it gives more movement than normal, so like we cannot change the stop loss of our trade immediately after a sideways movement because no stock moves in the same direction. He walks, sometimes takes a step back from the bridge and then moves ahead. Because this stock is a stock with movement, hence its pullbacks are also of the same type. For this reason, we can change the stop loss only after achieving 65% of the target.

Also see a no profit, no loss trade. In this trade, as soon as 1.3R was reached, I placed the stop loss at the entry point and then the big red candle hit that stop loss.

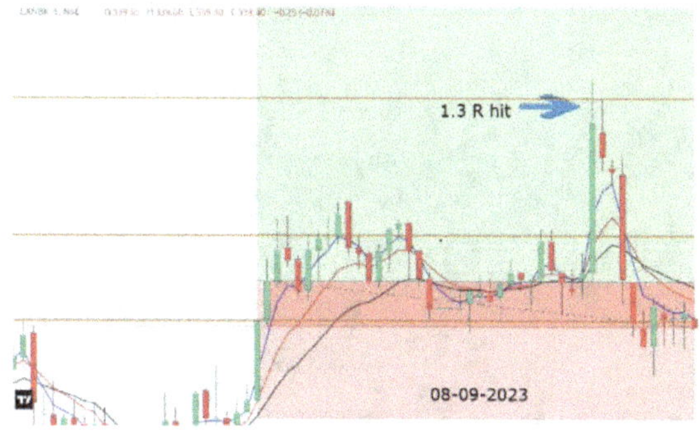

So, what I want to say is that even after getting 1.3 R in this strategy, we have to let go the profit. There is no way to take this small profit. And if you think that I will close the trade only after seeing the red candle. So, it is never possible to handle this strategy with habit and a lot of mistakes like this can happen.

2. **the stock goes up to 1:1.5RRR and reverses from there,** then we should exit after breaking 9 EMA.

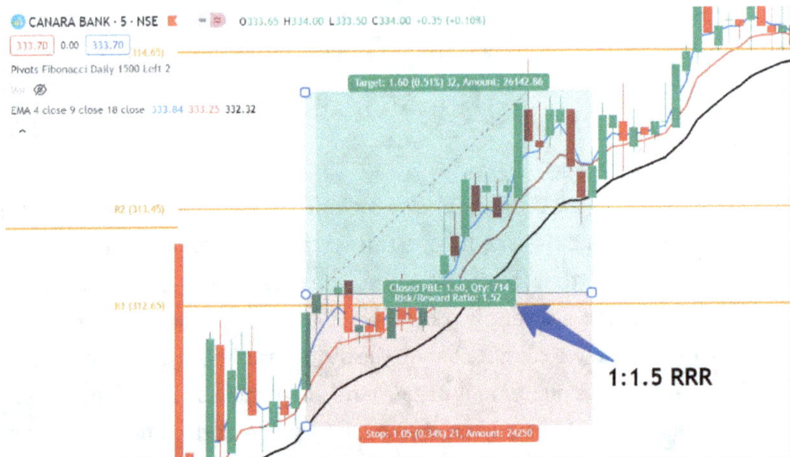

In this trade the stock is reversing from 1:1.5 RRR. So according to the rules, we should close the 9 EMA by breaking it and then exit the trade as shown in the chart below. In such a situation, the target 1:0.95 RRR has been achieved.

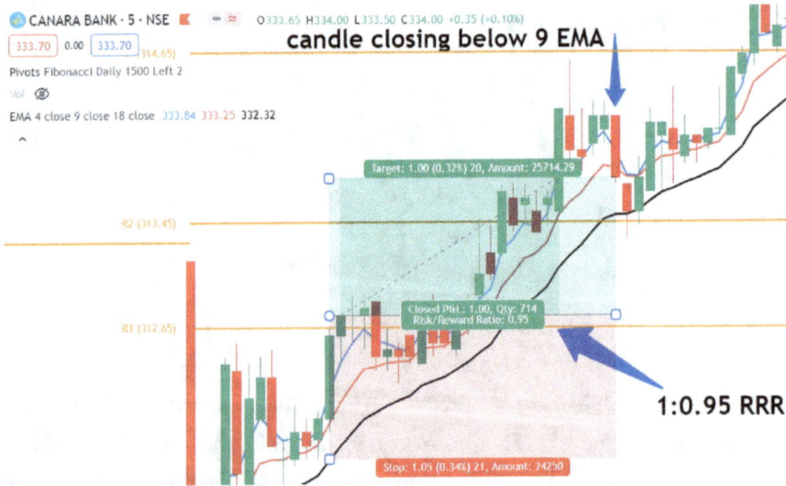

Now I am thinking that I should exit only if I got 1:1.5 RRR, then I would get more target. But we should not do this because we do not know from where the stock will reverse. We just have to follow the rules.

3. **If the stock is set at 1:2, 1:1.5 and the stop loss does not go anywhere.**

Then we have to exit the trade at 3:19. That is, just before the broker square off time. As done in the chart below. Which I call "Time Exit". In this trade, the stock price neither gave 1:2 target, nor gave stop loss, nor even went up to 1:1.5 RRR. Left in the middle and when square off time was at 3:20, he exited a minute earlier at 3:19. Then I got RRR of 1:0.69.

Just like we are making a profit of 0.69 R in the above trade, similarly there can be a loss also. When the Time Exit option appears, there may be a loss of some Rs. And sometimes no profit, no loss may also be found.

After taking the trade, rules are given according to the three possibilities mentioned above. Whom to follow. Whatever happens, don't deviate from the track. By anything I mean that apart from the possibilities given above, no new possibility is going to come. It means to say that follow the rules and do not exit the ongoing trade out of fear because

Look, one should not think that I will take the trade and if it goes to green then it is fine, but if it goes to red zone then I will come out of the trade. This should not be done. Because after taking the trade the following four things can happen.

1. Directly on target

2. Direct stop loss

3. Coming near the stop loss and then on the target

4. Coming near the target and then on the stop loss.

7. SECOND ENTRY:

If you get second or third entry, you can take it but if there are three reasons given below then you cannot take entry.

1. Second entry cannot be taken in the same candle in which exit was made in the first trade: It is very easy to understand this rule, if the trade is taken and the target is hit or the stop loss is hit, then the candle which was hit is the same candle. If another trade is available then do not take that trade. Like in the trade given below, the target of 1:2 is hit and a second entry is also found in the same candle. Pivot point is also broken. But according to the rules, if the target or candle giving stop loss gives a second entry, then we cannot take the trade.

Also see a trade with a stop loss.

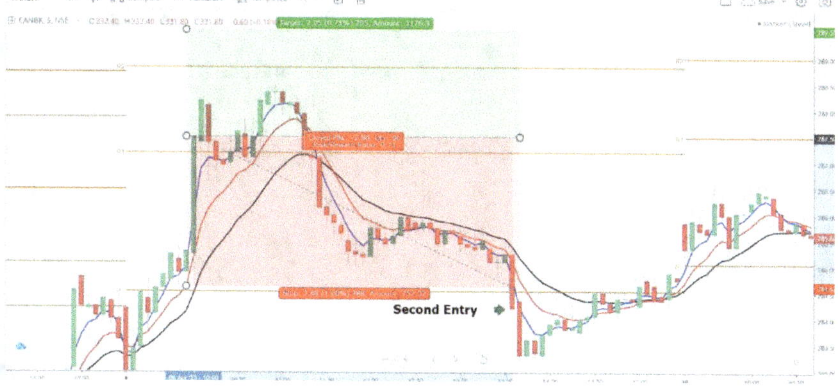

2. In the first trade, if the trade is found on the pivot point at which the stop loss is hit, then the second entry cannot be taken if the trade is found on the same pivot point.: These rules are also very simple, on the pivot point on which the stop loss is hit. Yes, no other entry can be taken on the same pivot point. Like on this day the 11:25 candle gave entry and within some time the stop loss was hit and again at the same pivot point the 2:30 candle gave entry which should not be taken. If taken, the stop loss would have been hit.

But if the target is changed then you can take another entry.

3. If you take a trade with a stop loss of more than 1% and the stop loss is hit, then you cannot enter another 1% trade on that day. If the target is hit in such a trade, then you can take it. Here I am talking only about trades with 1% stop loss. If the stop loss is less than 1% then you can take it.

8. PIVOT POINT CROSS:

It may take some time to understand these rules. If the price has crossed more than two times before the pivot point at which entry is being made, then the entry will not be valid. But let us see in what ways the entry is valid.

1. If there is a gap of at least 30 minutes between the first cross and the entry being received.

2. If the price makes a complete loop and comes out from the pivot point on any other side, even if there is not a gap of 30 minutes.

In the chart given below, entry is being seen at 10:15 minutes. But the entry is not valid. Why is it not valid? Price broke down the pivot point at 9:50 minutes and gave a breakout again in the next candle at 9:55. And after 15 minutes the 10:15 candle gives us entry. Now the pivot point has no value here. Therefore, the entry at 10:15 is not valid. But if the time gap of 15 minutes is 30 minutes or more then you can take entry. Because then the market structure or sentiment changes. Now the question is that how to measure this gap for the candle which comes back after breaking, like on this day the candle of 9:55 broke the pivot point and closed from above. Now the closing took place at the pivot point, then it is 10 o'clock. If we had already taken the time from 10:00, the time of that candle which broke the same pivot point again, which was 10:15 on this day, now there was a gap of 15 minutes between 10:00 and 10:15.

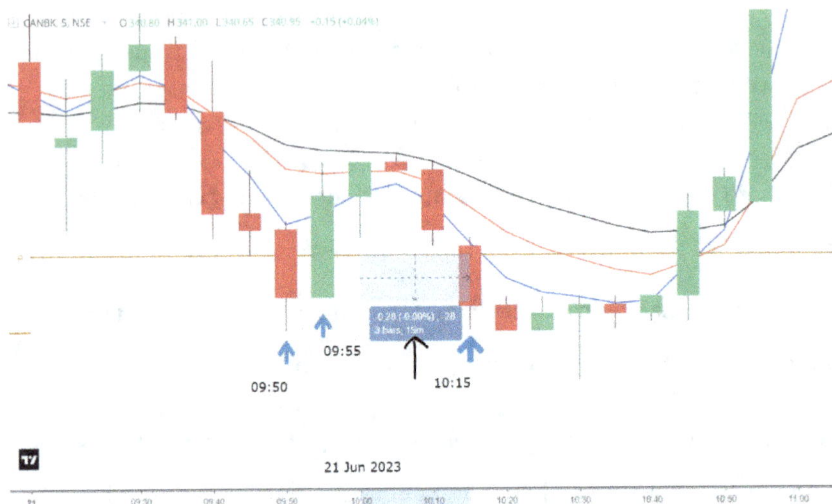

See, according to the rules on this day, if the time gap is more than 30 minutes then the entry is valid. In this the time gap is 55 minutes. That means the entry in this trade is valid.

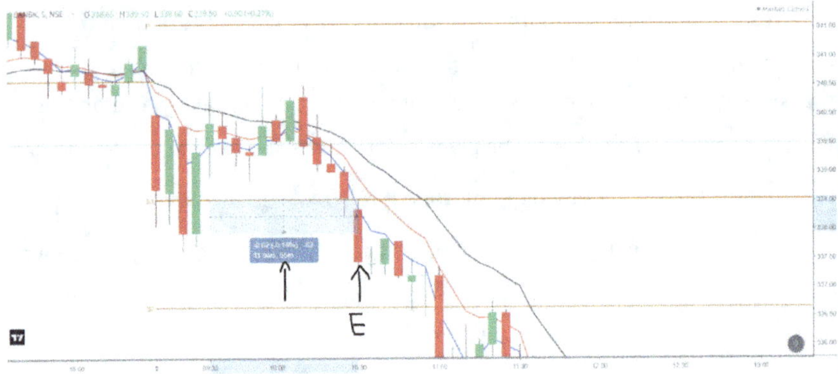

See, according to the rules, there should be a time gap of more than 30 minutes, but in this trade the time gap is only 20 minutes, yet why is the entry valid? The second reason for that is that the entry is valid. On this day, make a complete loop, go to the second pivot point, come back and enter again. To understand this, I have given numbers from one to four in the chart. Two to three prices move from one pivot point to another and then again break the same pivot point, that is, the price which touched other pivot points means the market sentiment has changed. The movement in the market has changed. Therefore, this entry is valid.

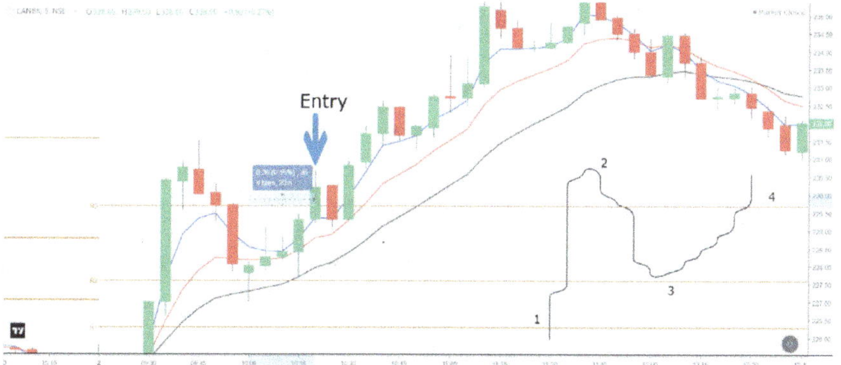

It may take some time to understand but it is not rocket science.

On this day, the 10 o'clock candle is giving entry but the breakout of the pivot point has taken place before the entry candle. Looking at the chart, at first glance it seems that there is an entry but the entry is not valid. Look carefully at the first candles from 10:00, the stock has become choppy. Even though it moved upwards, such entry is not valid according to this strategy.

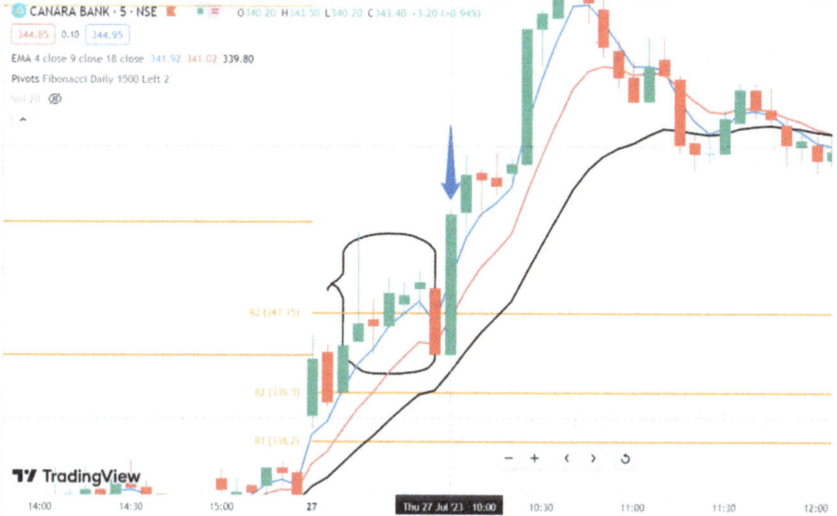

This day was very fun and confusing at the same time. Found the first trade and reversed from 1:1.5 R. It was as if I had to come out of the trade after closing below 9 EMA and the second candle itself broke the pivot points and gave another entry. In that a target of 1:2 was given. I know at first glance it seems that the pivot point was broken just a short time ago. So how did this entry become valid?

If you look carefully, the pivot point at 1:00 has not been broken. In the chart of tick size, it seems that the pivot point has been broken but it is not so. The price of the pivot point and the price of the candle at 1:00 are the same. What I want to say is that the candle at 1:00 did not break the pivot point and if it did not break then the candle at 1:35 is broken, which is a fresh entry.

9.IDENTIFYING VOLATILITY:

Stock All Ready has given more than 3% movement in any one direction, then if trade is found on that day, then it should be avoided. I know how difficult it is to avoid the trade given by the strategy but we have to do it.

This is because if the stock has already given a movement of 3% or more before giving entry and after that entry is received then there are more chances that an entry with 1% stop loss will be received and even after entering such a trade the stock will pull back. Even if he does it or not, to give the target the stock will have to move another 1.6%-2%, which the stock is all-ready for, so there is no sense in trading on such a day.

WHEN TO AVOID TRADES

Such entry should not be made, entry cannot be taken after looking at the 09:55 candle. It means that a very good buy sequence is visible and entry cannot be taken just by looking at it. Because the breakout has already occurred before two-three candles of 9:55.

Entry is to be taken in the trade only when the sequence is visible properly, by properly I mean it should be clearly visible. Look at the trade given below, the sequence of the next candle of the entry candle is not clearly visible, if I had entered this trade then the stop loss would have been hit. Do not enter the trade until a clear sequence is seen.

FOLLOW THE ENTRY STRATEGY

If due to any reason you are not able to take the trade as per the strategy, then you are getting another entry immediately, as shown in the chart given below. You need to decide which entry to take, as entry can occur more than once in the same position. There are three entries visible in this chart, but the first entry has been selected as the strategy entry because that is when the trade starts. If for some reason you are not able to take the first entry, then entry cannot be taken at the remaining two entry points, because the first entry has already taken place at the same time. You should enter and exit only after understanding the strategy. That means, even if you have not taken entry, the trade is going on as per the strategy. And suppose you delay your entry, then you will have to exit as per the trade of your strategy.

I did not take the strategy entry and then after some time the pivot point was broken again and I took the entry. However, in this trade I achieved the target but in the wrong way. "If you make money with wrong way then you don't understand right way" Now the problem is that what can happen when we make money in the wrong way once or twice. "You have to earn money with the right approach. Will happen" This topic has been discussed further.

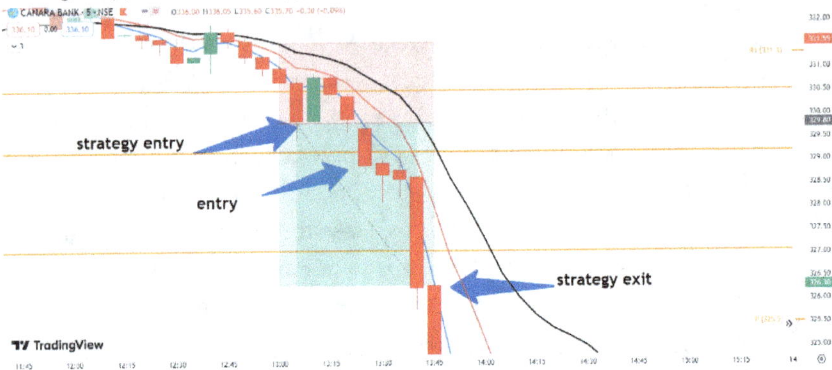

Entry: If the week of the same candle is four times or five times or more than the breakout, then the entry should be avoided because the entry candle is showing weakness, hence let us understand by looking at a chart.

In the above chart which is of 11 Oct 2023, the body of the entry candle is 0.03% and its week is 0.20%, which is more than six times the week of the candle, so we should not take such trade entry. If this trade had been taken then stop loss would have been given.

BACK TESTING

The day in which there is a break in the back testing data given below. Some reasons behind this: Trade may not have been found that day. As there will not be valid entries. The stock may have already moved more than 3%. There may be some reasons due to which entry in the trade may not be available as per the rules.

All the trades given below have "*" in them, those trades have stop loss above 1% and as per the rules, stop loss is set at 0.80%. And in some it is 0.81% instead of 0.80%, that is the tick size. And one more thing, I am not saying that this strategy gives 50%-60% win rate. I am saying that the probability of doing so is high.

No	Date	Entry Time	SL Size (in %)	Exit Time	Result (in R)
1	05/04/2022	10:45	0.64	11:25	2
2	06/04/2022	10:00	0.47	10:10	-1
3	06/04/2022	02:25	0.89	03:15	0.43
4	07/04/2022	12:05	0.99	12:50	-1
5	07/04/2022	01:15	0.58	01:45	2
6	11/04/2022	01:45	0.36	03:00	2
7	13/04/2022	11:05	0.80*	12:10	-1
8	18/04/2022	10:05	0.80*	11:20	1.21
9	19/04/2022	12:35	0.44	01:10	-1
10	19/04/2022	01:20	0.81*	02:55	0
					3.64

To show how the 10 trades appear in the charts given above, I am also putting charts of only 10 trades so that it becomes easier to see and understand the rest of the data.

In this trade, if 1:1.3 R was hit, then the stop loss was placed at the entry point, as if the trade has ended in no profit, no loss.

No	Date	Entry Time	SL Size (in %)	Exit Time	Result (in R)
1	22/04/2022	12:10	0.30	12:40	-1
2	22/04/2022	02:00	0.70	03:15	0.73
3	26/04/2022	11:00	0.70	03:15	0.97
4	27/04/2022	10:30	0.93	01:55	0
5	29/04/2022	11:45	0.49	11:55	-1
6	29/04/2022	02:05	0.69	03:05	2
7	04/05/2022	12:35	0.61	02:05	2
8	04/05/2022	02:25	0.80*	02:45	2
9	05/05/2022	01:40	0.77	02:45	0.48
10	06/05/2022	11:25	0.80*	11:35	-1
					5.18

No	Date	Entry Time	SL Size (in %)	Exit Time	Result (in R)
1	11/05/2022	10:30	0.81*	01:15	2
2	11/05/2022	02:00	0.80*	02:50	2
3	12/05/2022	10:05	0.81*	11:35	1.13
4	13/05/2022	11:05	0.96	02:10	-1
5	13/05/2022	02:40	0.80*	03:15	0.65
6	16/05/2022	11:40	0.77	12:20	-1
7	17/05/2022	09:55	0.71	11:25	-1
8	17/05/2022	12:35	0.60	01:55	2
9	18/05/2022	12:10	0.80	01:30	0.45
10	18/05/2022	02:45	0.74	03:15	0.28
					5.51

No	Date	Entry Time	SL Size (in %)	Exit Time	Result (in R)
1	19/05/2022	11:05	0.82*	02:10	2
2	20/05/2022	01:20	0.80*	01:40	-1
3	23/05/2022	02:30	0.80*	03:15	1.48
4	24/05/2022	02:30	0.92	03:15	0.26
5	25/05/2022	10:35	0.83	11:30	-1
6	25/05/2022	12:25	0.81	01:45	2
7	25/05/2022	02:40	0.85	03:15	0.88
8	26/05/2022	10:20	0.76	10:45	-1
9	26/05/2022	12:50	0.83	02:20	2
10	30/05/2022	11:35	0.62	01:00	2
					7.62

No	Date	Entry Time	SL Size (in %)	Exit Time	Result (in R)
1	01/06/2022	01:10	0.51	03:00	0
2	02/06/2022	11:45	0.56	12:20	-1
3	02/06/2022	01:05	0.38	02:05	0.87
4	06/06/2022	12:55	0.59	01:35	-1
5	07/06/2022	10:10	0.80*	10:35	-1
6	07/06/2022	11:45	0.62	02:25	0.80
7	08/06/2022	10:35	0.80*	01:30	-1
8	09/06/2022	10:45	0.70	02:10	1.45
9	10/06/2022	11:00	0.48	11:25	-1
10	14/06/2022	10:15	0.55	11:10	2
					0.12

No	Date	Entry Time	SL Size (in %)	Exit Time	Result (in R)
1	14/06/2022	12:20	0.68	02:20	0.89
2	16/06/2022	11:20	0.93	01:00	2
3	17/06/2022	02:20	0.72	02:35	-1
4	20/06/2022	10:30	0.80*	11:40	-1
5	21/06/2022	12:45	0.78	03:15	0.96
6	22/06/2022	01:35	0.72	02:05	-1
7	23/06/2022	10:25	0.76	11:50	-1
8	23/06/2022	12:20	0.80*	01:30	0
9	24/06/2022	01:00	0.59	03:15	0
10	27/06/2022	11:05	0.63	02:15	-1
					-1.15

No	Date	Entry Time	SL Size (in %)	Exit Time	Result (in R)
1	30/06/2022	11:00	0.62	01:15	0.85
2	30/06/2022	01:55	0.36	02:30	2
3	01/07/2022	01:40	0.54	02:30	-1
4	04/07/2022	10:50	0.80*	03:15	0.40
5	05/07/2022	12:05	0.39	01:05	0.60
6	05/07/2022	01:55	0.87	03:15	0
7	06/07/2022	11:15	0.32	12:00	0.42
8	06/07/2022	12:40	0.47	02:00	-1
9	11/07/2022	09:55	0.80*	11:10	-1
10	12/07/2022	10:40	0.96	11:35	-1
					0.27

No	Date	Entry Time	SL Size (in %)	Exit Time	Result (in R)
1	14/07/2022	10:25	0.89	12:10	2
2	15/07/2022	12:15	0.91	02:35	-1
3	18/07/2022	12:10	0.57	01:25	0.92
4	18/07/2022	01:35	0.47	02:45	2
5	19/07/2022	10:05	0.80*	02:30	2
6	20/07/2022	10:35	0.54	11:35	-1
7	21/07/2022	10:45	0.36	11:05	2
8	21/07/2022	11:20	0.80*	01:15	2
9	22/07/2022	12:55	0.82	01:10	-1
10	25/07/2022	11:25	0.67	12:40	-1
					6.92

No	Date	Entry Time	SL Size (in %)	Exit Time	Result (in R)
1	26/07/2022	09:55	0.97	03:15	-0.10
2	27/07/2022	10:00	0.52	10:30	0.25
3	27/07/2022	01:25	0.53	02:30	2
4	28/07/2022	02:30	0.60	03:00	-1
5	29/07/2022	10:30	0.67	02:40	1.10
6	02/08/2022	10:20	0.80*	11:00	2
7	03/08/2022	10:30	0.60	10:40	-1
8	04/08/2022	10:35	0.70	11:00	2
9	05/08/2022	10:25	0.80*	01:05	-1
10	08/08/2022	02:20	0.79	02:40	-1
					3.25

No	Date	Entry Time	SL Size (in %)	Exit Time	Result (in R)
1	12/08/2022	01:10	0.41	01:30	-1
2	12/08/2022	02:35	0.87	03:15	-0.10
3	17/08/2022	01:00	0.89	01:45	0.76
4	19/08/2022	11:00	0.68	11:40	2
5	22/08/2022	01:10	0.74	03:15	0.61
6	23/08/2022	01:25	0.75	03:15	1.12
7	24/08/2022	02:30	0.46	03:15	1.52
8	26/08/2022	01:05	0.64	03:15	0.94
9	30/08/2022	01:25	0.89	03:15	-0.10
10	05/09/2022	10:00	0.45	10:35	0
					5.75

No	Date	Entry Time	SL Size (in %)	Exit Time	Result (in R)
1	06/09/2022	10:15	0.80*	11:25	-1
2	06/09/2022	11:35	0.82	02:40	-1
3	07/09/2022	10:35	0.52	03:15	0.55
4	08/09/2022	11:35	0.29	12:15	-1
5	08/09/2022	12:55	0.39	13:15	-1
6	09/09/2022	10:25	0.34	10:30	2
7	09/09/2022	12:00	0.82	03:15	0.63
8	12/09/2022	01:45	0.41	02:55	2
9	14/09/2022	09:55	0.49	11:05	-1
10	14/09/2022	12:05	0.48	12:25	2
					2.18

No	Date	Entry Time	SL Size (in %)	Exit Time	Result (in R)
1	15/09/2022	10:45	0.87	01:10	-1
2	16/09/2022	10:10	0.80*	01:00	2
3	19/09/2022	11:10	0.80*	02:20	-1
4	20/09/2022	10:45	0.46	11:25	-1
5	21/09/2022	11:50	0.89	02:10	-1
6	22/09/2022	10:05	0.81*	11:00	0.86
7	27/09/2022	02:25	0.82*	03:15	0.39
8	06/10/2022	02:35	0.66	03:15	0.13
9	07/10/2022	11:30	0.39	12:10	-1
10	07/10/2022	12:40	0.68	03:00	2
					0.38

No	Date	Entry Time	SL Size (in %)	Exit Time	Result (in R)
1	10/10/2022	11:20	0.48	12:45	2
2	10/10/2022	02:00	0.42	03:10	-1
3	11/10/2022	12:35	0.74	03:15	0.79
4	13/10/2022	10:05	0.72	02:10	0
5	19/10/2022	01:00	0.37	01:10	-1
6	20/10/2022	09:55	0.80*	11:15	0
7	28/10/2022	01:05	0.54	02:00	0.75
8	31/10/2022	10:05	0.75	10:75	-1
9	31/10/2022	11:35	0.64	03:15	0.51
10	01/11/2022	11:55	**0.24**	01:05	5
					6.05

No	Date	Entry Time	SL Size (in %)	Exit Time	Result (in R)
1	02/11/2022	11:40	0.29	11:55	0
2	04/11/2022	10:50	0.42	01:10	2
3	09/11/2022	10:00	0.61	10:55	0.53
4	09/11/2022	12:05	0.85	12:30	-1
5	09/11/2022	02:05	0.98	03:15	-0.35
6	10/11/2022	10:30	0.81*	12:25	2
7	14/11/2022	12:10	0.31	01:00	2
8	15/11/2022	01:20	0.55	03:15	1.18
9	16/11/2022	10:05	0.68	10:45	-1
10	16/11/2022	01:00	0.39	02:20	2
					7.36

No	Date	Entry Time	SL Size (in %)	Exit Time	Result (in R)
1	17/11/2022	01:30	**0.20**	02:55	0.92
2	21/11/2022	10:15	0.44	11:00	2
3	21/11/2022	11:05	0.80*	03:15	0.42
4	22/11/2022	01:05	**0.22**	02:20	5
5	24/11/2022	12:00	0.26	01:20	-1
6	25/11/2022	11:10	0.73	02:30	1.18
7	29/11/2022	10:50	0.40	12:55	-1
8	30/11/2022	10:35	0.41	11:25	2
9	30/11/2022	11:40	0.68	12:55	1.15
10	01/12/2022	10:20	0.62	01:50	-1
					9.67

No	Date	Entry Time	SL Size (in %)	Exit Time	Result (in R)
1	02/12/2022	10:20	0.65	10:55	-1
2	02/12/2022	11:50	0.64	03:15	0.18
3	05/12/2022	02:05	0.60	03:15	0.97
4	06/12/2022	02:00	0.61	03:15	0.54
5	07/12/2022	10:40	0.84	11:40	0.50
6	08/12/2022	11:05	0.95	11:41	2
7	08/12/2022	01:30	0.77	02:05	-1
8	09/12/2022	12:45	0.81*	02:10	2
9	12/12/2022	02:00	0.39	02:20	-1
10	13/12/2022	10:50	0.34	11:45	0
					3.19

No	Date	Entry Time	SL Size (in %)	Exit Time	Result (in R)
1	13/12/2022	02:30	0.78	03:15	0.13
2	14/12/2022	11:45	0.23	11:50	-1
3	14/12/2022	01:40	0.49	01:50	-1
4	15/12/2022	11:30	0.55	11:50	2
5	15/12/2022	02:45	0.77	03:15	0.24
6	16/12/2022	10:00	0.81*	12:50	0.77
7	19/12/2022	10:40	0.76	03:15	1.19
8	21/12/2022	12:10	0.80*	01:40	2
9	21/12/2022	01:50	0.80*	02:05	-1
10	22/12/2022	10:30	0.77	11:15	-1
					2.33

No	Date	Entry Time	SL Size (in %)	Exit Time	Result (in R)
1	23/12/2022	10:10	0.80*	10:55	2
2	28/12/2022	10:00	0.80*	11:10	2
3	30/12/2022	10;20	0.80*	02:20	2
4	02/01/2023	02:45	0.50	03:48	-0.22
5	03/01/2023	12:15	0.49	01:40	-1
6	04/01/2023	09:55	0.80*	12:20	0.86
7	05/01/2023	10:05	0.80*	11:00	-1
8	06/01/2023	12:40	0.82	03:00	0.87
9	09/01/2023	11:25	0.80*	01:45	-1
10	10/01/2023	10:30	0.87	12:50	2
					6.51

No	Date	Entry Time	SL Size (in %)	Exit Time	Result (in R)
1	12/01/2023	11:10	0.55	03:15	-0.50
2	13/01/2023	12:45	0.41	01:40	2
3	13/01/2023	01:50	0.80*	03:15	0.42
4	17/01/2023	12:20	0.44	12:30	2
5	17/01/2023	12:35	0.80*	01:35	0.53
6	18/01/2023	01:30	0.43	02:14	-1
7	19/01/2023	10:50	0.31	11:00	-1
8	19/01/2023	01:05	0.42	03:15	0.69
9	23/01/2023	11:20	**0.23**	12:05	5
10	24/01/2023	11:00	0.64	12:40	1
					9.14

No	Date	Entry Time	SL Size (in %)	Exit Time	Result (in R)
1	25/01/2023	10:10	0.80*	11:10	2
2	30/01/2023	01:40	0.80*	02:00	-1
3	31/01/2023	10:30	0.80*	01:20	2
4	01/02/2023	12:55	0.80*	10:05	-1
5	03/02/2023	12:15	0.68	03:15	0
6	07/02/2023	10:30	0.69	12:35	-1
7	08/02/2023	10:46	0.80*	10:55	-1
8	13/02/2023	10:00	0.80*	01:15	1.15
9	14/02/2023	12:10	0.29	01:10	2
10	15/02/2023	10:20	0.46	11:45	0
					3.15

All ready 4% move had arrived on 27th. So, no trade.

No	Date	Entry Time	SL Size (in %)	Exit Time	Result (in R)
1	15/02/2023	01:10	**0.19**	01:15	-1
2	16/02/2023	01:20	0.28	02:25	-1
3	17/02/2023	12:55	0.47	01:20	0
4	20/02/2023	11:25	0.60	03:15	1.22
5	21/02/2023	12:20	0.91	03:15	1.62
6	24/02/2023	11:40	0.63	03:00	0
7	27/02/2023	11:10	0.80*	03:15	0.22
8	28/02/2023	10:10	0.56	03:10	0.97
9	28/02/2023	02:10	0.65	02:25	-1
10	01/03/2023	10:05	0.81*	02:00	2
					3.05

No	Date	Entry Time	SL Size (in %)	Exit Time	Result (in R)
1	02/03/2023	12:25	0.45	12:35	-1
2	06/03/2023	12:05	0.34	01:05	-1
3	08/03/2023	12:30	0.34	12:45	-1
4	08/03/2023	02:20	0.73	03:15	0
5	09/03/2023	10:05	0.46	10:35	-1
6	13/03/2023	12:55	0.80*	02:50	2
7	14/03/2023	10;30	0.80*	12:25	-1
8	15/03/2023	12:50	0.45	01:40	-1
9	16/03/2023	11:00	0.80*	11:15	-1
10	17/03/2023	10:15	0.78	11:40	1.18
					-3.82

No	Date	Entry Time	SL Size (in %)	Exit Time	Result (in R)
1	17/03/2023	12:15	0.56	12:45	-1
2	17/03/2023	13:50	0.93	03:15	-0.10
3	20/03/2023	10:25	0.75	10:40	-1
4	21/03/2023	10:40	0.59	11:50	-1
5	21/03/2023	12:45	0.67	02:50	2
6	22/03/2023	12:50	**0.23**	01:25	-1
7	23/03/2023	02:40	0.49	03:05	2
8	24/03/2023	10:25	0.87	03:15	1.65
9	28/03/2023	10:35	0.38	11:40	0
10	28/03/2023	02:05	0.34	02:30	-1
					0.55

No	Date	Entry Time	SL Size (in %)	Exit Time	Result (in R)
1	29/03/2023	10:20	0.54	02:00	2
2	29/03/2023	02:05	0.75	03:15	0.19
3	03/04/2023	11:45	0.44	03:15	0
4	05/04/2023	09:55	0.76	03:15	-0.20
5	06/04/2023	10:00	0.80*	11:45	-1
6	10/04/2023	11:05	0.33	12:20	0
7	13/04/2023	01:15	0.43	02:05	2
8	17/04/2023	11:05	0.48	11:40	2
9	17/04/2023	02:10	0.52	03:15	0.23
10	18/04/2023	01:35	0.74	02:25	-1
					4.22

No	Date	Entry Time	SL Size (in %)	Exit Time	Result (in R)
1	19/04/2023	01:30	0.41	01:55	2
2	21/04/2023	10:00	0.66	02:55	-1
3	21/04/2023	02:30	0.78	03:15	-0.60
4	24/04/2023	11:35	0.42	01:55	2
5	27/04/2023	10:05	0.32	02:00	-1
6	02/05/2023	11:15	0.64	03:15	-0.60
7	03/05/2023	11:45	0.35	01:25	-1
8	04/05/2023	11:15	0.69	03:15	1.25
9	05/05/2023	11:45	0.95	03:15	0.85
10	08/05/2023	10:10	0.80*	01:15	2
					3.90

2. RISK MANAGEMENT

If you want to know how to manage risk? If you know this then you can skip this part.

If not then we will have to follow some rules for that.

Risk management is a very big subject. It is difficult to understand completely in one go, but after reading it completely, you will be able to manage your risk very easily. You may feel that this is too much, but believe me, following some rules will manage your risk. And yes, I have spoken directly to the point on this issue.

RISK PER TRADE

Trade at risk, which is the price of how much money you are willing to risk in a trade.

RPT means how much money you are willing to risk on a trade, and RTP is used to accurately measure this. When you trade, you should try to risk only 2% to 3% of your capital on each trade. This means if you have a capital of Rs 100000 then you should take a risk of Rs 3000 while trading. With this you can make a loss of only Rs 3000 in one trade. If you take more risk than this, your capital may be at risk.

An important thing here is that if you are new then you should keep only 2% risk in trading in the beginning. After good gains in trading, you can think of risking 3% of your capital.

This means it's important to understand how much money you can afford to risk. How much capital you have, and how much money you are willing to risk, is important for savings and security. This method of risk management ensures the safety of your capital, so that you have the ability to withstand potential losses.

In this strategy you can trade at 3% risk, but there are some conditions. You will have to take all the trades given by this strategy and follow the rules completely. One more thing to keep in mind is that for every 10 trades which are out-come, there should not be a loss of more than 20% of the trading capital. That is, if 6 out of 10 trades are incurring a loss of more than R, then there can be two issues, we will come directly to the solution. Look carefully at those ten treads, there might have been some mistake somewhere. So, work on that mistake and follow the trading rules because the rules are designed to execute the strategy better and if it is not so. So will take a break in trading for a week. You will not make any trades, you will not look at any charts and yes, you will not work on any other strategy. Will take only and only breaks. I know it is a difficult task, but it has to be done for trading capital.

HIT RATE

Win rat means how many trades you win. If you make 100 trades and you succeed in making money in 60 trades, your win rate will be 60%.

Imagine you have a toy and you played it 10 times. When you win 6 times, your win rate will be 60%. This means that 6 out of 10 times you won.

Looking at your win rate lets you know how successfully your trading strategy is working. However, note that the win rate is only one part. It needs to be considered along with other measurements such as average winning trade size, average losing trade size, and risk-reward ratio to get a complete picture of the success of your trades.

Your hit rate should be at least 50%, that is, 5 out of 10 trades should be correct, only then you will be in profit and the important thing is that out of 10, it may be that 7 or 8 of your trades will be correct, but if you go right, what is your risk and reward? This is also very important.

RISK AND REWARD

That means you keep 300 Rs at risk in the trade and against it at the time of profit you take only 300 rs and it is called 1:1. In another way, you know that your stop loss in the trade is 2 rupees and if you exit the trade with 4 rupees then your risk and reward is said to be 1:2.

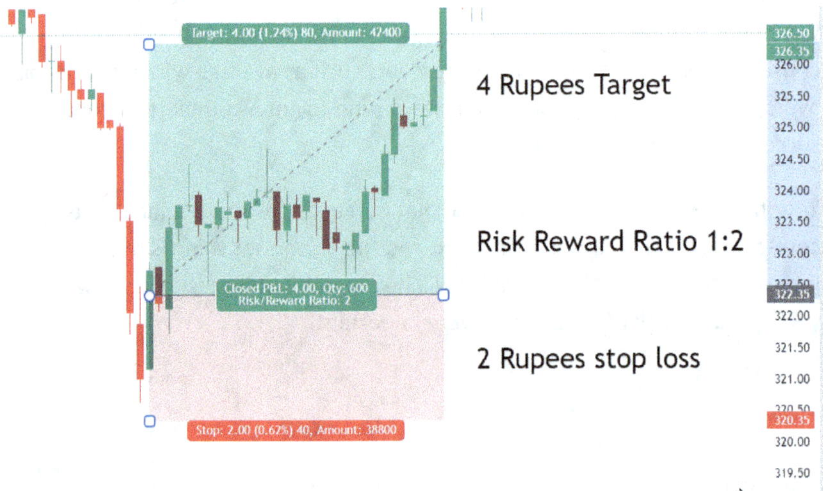

That means whenever you trade, the amount of reward compared to your risk is very important. You have to take a reward of at least 1:2 compared to your risk. Only then will you be able to make profits.

hit rate (win rate) is given in [%] and risk and reward are given in [:]

	20%	30%	40%	50%	60%
1:1	Not Profitable	Not Profitable	Not Profitable	**Break Even**	Profitable
1:2	Not Profitable	Not Profitable	Profitable	Profitable	Profitable
1:3	Not Profitable	Profitable	Profitable	Profitable	Profitable
1:4	**Break Even**	Profitable	Profitable	Profitable	Profitable
1:5	Profitable	Profitable	Profitable	Profitable	Profitable

You will be able to make profit only after seeing your hit rate (win rate) and the risk and reward in front of it. You will understand this by looking at the box given above.

POSITION SIZING

This means that the quantity of shares that you take while taking a trade has to be decided. There is a formula for how to do it. Quantity = Risk Per Trade/Stop Loss in Rupees

This formula will tell you how much quantity you have to take while taking a trade. Let us understand with an example, suppose we have to buy SBI whose price is Rs 300 and our stop loss is kept at Rs 297, then what will be our quantity in this case? Trade at risk is 300 rupees, according to 10000 capital, 3% = 300 rupees and stop loss is 300-297=3, so our quantity will be 100 {300/3=100}

According to this formula, we do not have to buy quantity above 100.

Summary

We just have to follow these rules. Complete risk management will be covered in this.

Risk per trade:

According to the capital, only 2% to 3% has to be risked in a trade.

Win rate:

Must be at least 50% (out of 10 trades, at least 5 trades must be correct.)

Risk & reward ratio:

Take 1:2 (If stop loss is Rs 2 then target should be taken at least Rs 4.)

Position size:

quantity = risk per trade / stop loss in rupees (The quantity has to be decided according to this formula only.)

EDGE

To get an edge in trading, you should know about some things. If you want to know about RTP, Win Rate, RRR which we learned above.

But the most important thing is that your win rate should be at least 50%, that is, 5 out of 10 trades should be correct and your risk to reward ratio should be at least 1:2, only then you will be profitable.

Now at least 5 of your 10 trades should be correct.

Let us understand with an example. Suppose you have a capital of Rs 10000 and you have to keep only 3% risk per trade, accordingly you can keep Rs 300 at risk in one trade.

Your 5 trades are wrong and 5 trades are right. When you are wrong, you make a loss of Rs. 300 and when you are right, you make Rs. 600 in profit.

300 * 5 = -1500

600 * 5 = 3000

profit 1500

We are not counting the commission here because when your capital is more than Rs 1 lakh then this commission seems very less in comparison to the profit. The only edge here is +1500.

You might be finding the profit of Rs 1500 very less but the capital is also less and anyway, according to the percentage (%) of Rs 1500 capital of Rs 10000 in 10 trades, the profit is 15% and in every 10 trades, your capital should increase by 15%. Considered to have a very good ROI.

All the points or formulas given above depend on each other. Your trading edge depends on your strategy. The strategy may not give 1:1 RRR but the win rent may be higher. It is possible that your win rate may be low but RRR may be high, it depends on the strategy. Look, I am not confusing you at all. According to the strategy, just by looking at your win rate and RRR, you can know whether the strategy has edge or not.

TRADE TAKING PROCESS

You must have understood all the things given above, but still for the sake of clarity how to use it. So, let's take an example.

Suppose the account size is Rs 1 lakh. Now getting entry in trade.

In the chart given above, E means where short entry is being received. So, we will go to tools and select short position option, because sell entry is available here. Then where the entry is being made. Keep it on and then go to its settings.

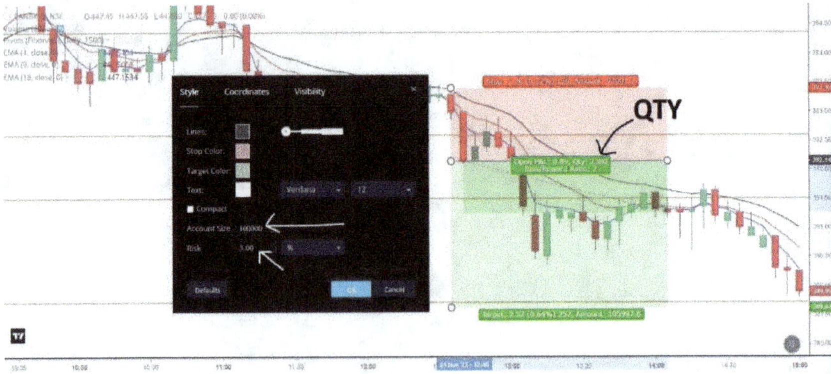

Account size should be for winning, here it is one lakh, then just below that Risk is 3% of total trading capital then ok, after that whatever qty of lion we have to take according to RPT, ok will show here 2380 qty. Now place an order in the market and put a stop loss, the work is done. **Then we have to wait and follow the rules.**

3. MAINTAIN

Look, the most difficult part can be anyone, it can be difficult to follow what, but I don't know because everyone has different style of working. For some, the position sizing part of risk management may be difficult to maintain, while for others it may be about making the right entry or exit.

Look, the position sizing part of risk management should be maintained by yourself and left to VIN rate and RRR strategies. Leaving it to the strategy means that the rules of the strategy have to be followed properly. We can never be perfect in the stock market. Never!! We are learners and earners but we cannot say that I am expert or expert in stock market.

Me: It is not possible that you do not take trades with stop loss and take only target giving trades.

Bhargav: No one knows which trade out of ten trades will give the target or which trade will give the stop loss and there is no way to know this. If we get a trade according to the strategy, we will have to take that trade. If we don't do this, we will become emotional after a few trades and will start breaking the rules. Because the strategy gave a trade but we did not take it. Now two things will happen here.

1. **It is fine if the trade gives a stop loss.** You will be happy that it is good that I did not take this trade, I saved one stop loss. Now you will not be able to take the next trade that the strategy will give you or you will take it out of fear and it is possible that you will be taken out of the trade even before the trade gives you the target.

2. **Trade gave target.** Now you will be sad about this. Should have taken this trade. Now you will take any trade and it is possible that there may be loss in it too and there may also be over trading. Over trading is poison for capital.

Personally, I believe that if one rule is broken, then how many more rules do we break consciously. I have seen that everything goes well until the first rule is broken. But when one rule is broken then it becomes very difficult to maintain the other rules. And what we do after that, we don't know ourselves.

I have seen and I have also done this many times, whenever the strategy did not give us any trade for a day or two and we did not trade, we felt bored. Because we are bored, we take any trade which has no setup, no reason, no logic, no sense. Meaning we took the trade just like that or we thought the stock would go up. We just take trades on the peg which we should not take.

WHAT IS THE EMOTION AFTER ACHIEVING THE TARGET AND WHAT SHOULD BE KEPT?

So generally, a trader thinks in two ways or we can say that two types of emotions come.

1. The stock reaches the target and goes back from there or stops there.

2. The stock goes beyond the target (which invites greed)

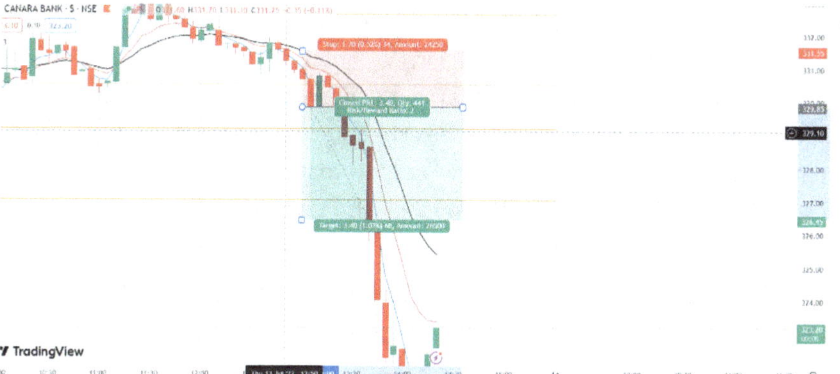

The target given in this trade was a move of 1%. And from there we have given a target of more than 1% which we could not achieve by setting a system target of 1:2 RRR. I say look at such a chart.

The target was given within 10 minutes of entry which was a move of 1%. And from the same we have given a target of 1% which we could not achieve by setting a system target of 1:2 RRR.

Now we will talk about leaving some money, some target on the screen, what does it mean? This simply means that when our decided target is achieved then we should come out of our trade. However, as per the rules the target should be set in the system itself. That is because sometimes it happens that the stock will move very fast and it is possible that it will go back after making a week and sometimes it will happen that it will give two times or even three times more than the target but oh movement. Will not be able to take it. And we will have to leave that movement. If this is not done then it is possible that in one such big movement a big target will be achieved but then this will happen every time whenever you get a trade you will expect that this time too you will get a big target and will break the rules and then also a normal target. It will be difficult to take. And it is possible that even the normal target may not be achieved, then rules will be broken again and again and setup or strategy will have no importance.

But still there will be some people who will be smart, they will think that I am sitting in front of the computer screen, when the target price comes and if it moves in the direction of my trade, then I will hold the trade and if it stops there, Then I will immediately exit the trade and book profit. By doing this thing, you will definitely get a target higher than the normal target once or twice, but it will happen that in some trades you will not be able to take even the normal target and will make mistakes and break rules after rules and then the irregularity will increase and the same strategy. Will have no importance.

MISS TRADE

Once it happened with me that the strategy gave a trade but due to some reason, I could not take the entry, so I thought, when the stock comes back to the same price at which the entry was made, then I will take the entry in the trade. So, I placed the order in the system and what happened was that within five minutes the stock gave a target of 1.5 R and my order was still pending. And I left it like this, now according to the strategy, if the stock reverses after getting the target at 1.5 R, then I have to close the price above 9 EMA, only then I have to do manual exit. That means, according to the strategy, I should make it out at break even.

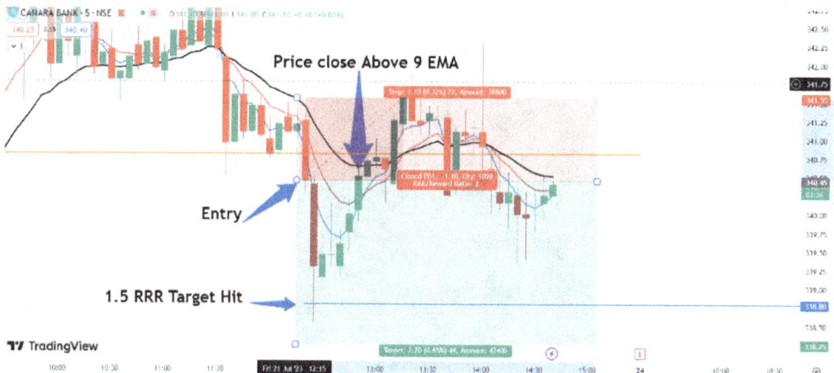

So, the strategy has also said exit. Now I should not take entry in the trade. But the order I placed got executed and I entered the trade and the stop loss was hit.

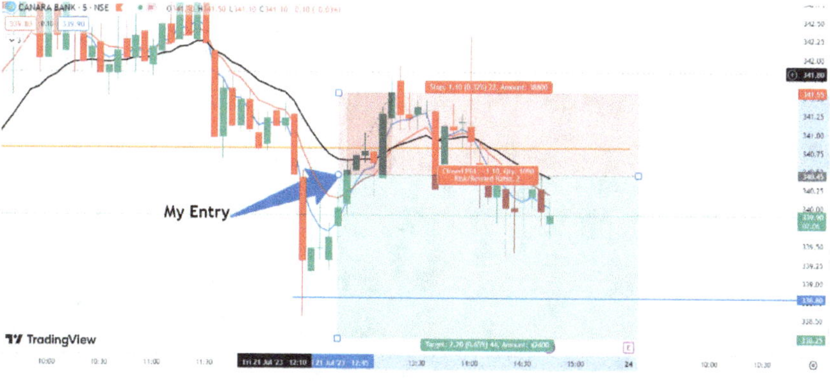

What this means is that I may have missed entry in the trade due to any reason but I have to follow the entry and exit strategy given by me.

Trust the strategy. Sometimes such trades are also found in which the meter meters at other places are saying something else, such as based on the price action.

I took the trade, the stock went sideways for a long time and in the 2:15 minute candle, I felt that the upper side has broken out and now the stop loss will be hit. I also felt scared but I did not exit out of fear. I trusted the strategy and I followed the rules. Target of 1:2 RRR achieved.

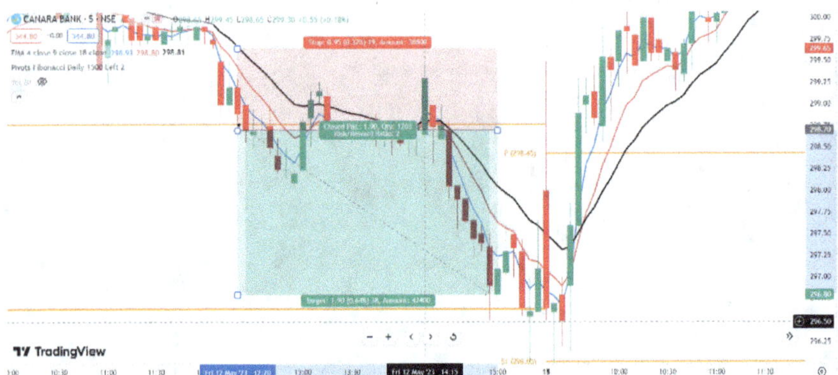

And sometimes it has happened that the stop loss was saved by a few rupees and the target was given from there. This is clearly visible in the chart given below. Stop loss was left at 0.15 paise and target was given from there.

They're come such days when the stock reverses after taking such a good entry. Look at the chart below, it did not come into the green zone even once.

The most painful thing for a trader is when the next candle of the entry candle gives a stop loss. As if someone had immediately proved our point wrong. It is difficult to rely on strategy at such times.

Some days are like this also. By giving stop loss, you give the complete target. As in the chart given below, the stop loss was hit shortly after entry and then the journey towards the target was completed.

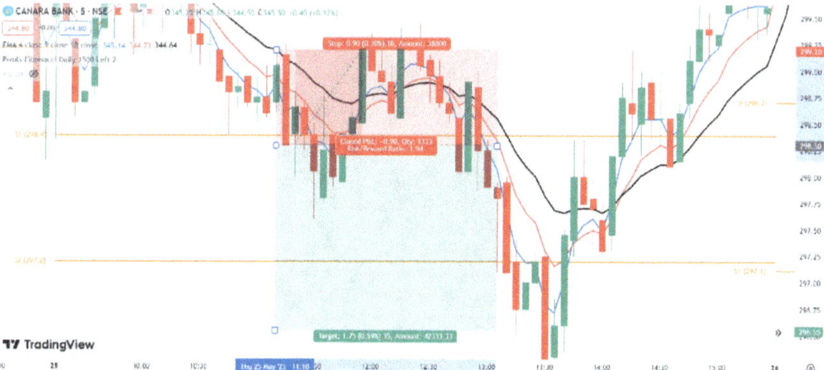

And whenever such stop loss is hit and immediately after that the stock goes in the same direction, then we feel that the operator got our stop loss hit but the thinking needs to be changed a little. Understand one thing, the operator did not say that you take the trade, he did not say that you set a stop loss here. The operator did not force anyone to do trading. You are taking trades of your own free will. You don't know how to work properly, why blame others for that, we have to accept ourselves. We have to accept ourselves as we are, only then we will change our way of working and will be able to work on it.

But still, I say that you should trust your strategy. And sometimes the trade will be missed, we will get a little late entry or due to some reason we will not be able to take the trade and then the same trade will give a good target then oh we will have to let it go, oh we will have to leave it, if we pay more attention to that then the coming ones will It may affect the tread.

NO SETUP, NO TRADE

In trading, if you are watching the market, anywhere on mobile, laptop, and are not getting entry in any trade, then you are not taking the trade, then you should understand that there is a psychology factor in trading, which is You have understood the emotional factor. If you can wait for your setup, entry of your strategy and nothing is happening to you or you are not worried that I have to take a trade, then you have great clarity in your mind regarding the strategy. There is trust in the strategy, and this trust helps in making money in the market. Because this strategy does not give entry in daily trade, does not give target in every trade it gives, and there is no such strategy in this world which gives daily trade and gives target in every trade. We have to work keeping the age in mind.

If the strategy gives entry, we will have to take the entry, whether the target is achieved or the stop loss is another matter. And by the way, we do not need to know what is going to happen next, whatever is going to happen will happen, we just have to do our work, follow the rules made by us. Given by give we have to make the strategy sharper.

Loss

According to me there are two types of losses.

1. Internal Loss: The loss given by the strategy, that is, we can say that we have no control over it. for example

- The strategy gave a stop loss. (If the strategy gives two losing streaks together then we should take a break of one week and not watch the market in those two weeks, although it is very common to have two losing streaks together, but I do not think that the strategy should give two losing streaks together. Will give a losing streak, yes but the loss should be the loss of the strategy, not that you broke the rules and got loss. But still if this happens then definitely take a break. Look, anything can happen in the market, but if you survive the hard days and survive, you will make money in the team.)

- Difference between stop loss trigger price and order executed price: Let us understand with an example. In this trade, I placed the stop loss at 344.05 and mostly the trade is cut at the price at which the stop loss is placed. But in some cases, the price moves so fast that the price goes above the stop loss price. Same thing happened in this case when instead of coming at 344.05 the stock went straight to 344.20. Now what happened was that when my order went to the market, there were not as many sellers at Rs 344.20 as the quantity I had. I have 1554 quantity of which some orders were placed at

344.20 and some at 344.25.

BUY **CANBK** NSE   COMPLETE

Trade ID	Time	Exch. time	Exch. id	Product	Qty	Avg. price
2536424	11:51:28	11:51:28	1000000015165124	MIS	169	344.2
2536425	11:51:28	11:51:28	1000000015165124	MIS	1	344.2
2536426	11:51:28	11:51:28	1000000015165124	MIS	25	344.2
2536427	11:51:28	11:51:28	1000000015165124	MIS	627	344.2
2536428	11:51:28	11:51:28	1000000015165124	MIS	145	344.2
2536429	11:51:28	11:51:28	1000000015165124	MIS	111	344.2
2536430	11:51:28	11:51:28	1000000015165124	MIS	2	344.2
2536431	11:51:28	11:51:28	1000000015165124	MIS	100	344.25
2536432	11:51:28	11:51:28	1000000015165124	MIS	25	344.25
2536433	11:51:28	11:51:28	1000000015165124	MIS	349	344.25

So, the average price came to 344.22 which is 0.17 paise more than the stop loss I had placed. That means a loss of 1554*0.17=264.18 over which we have no control.

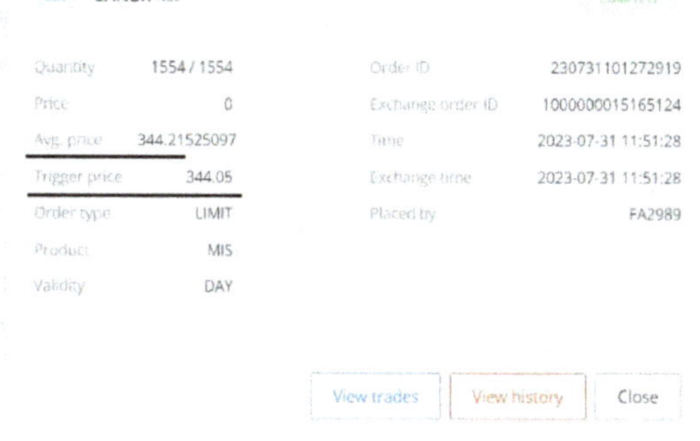

BUY **CANBK** NSE   COMPLETE

Quantity	1554 / 1554	Order ID	230731101272919
Price	0	Exchange order ID	1000000015165124
Avg. price	344.21525097	Time	2023-07-31 11:51:28
Trigger price	344.05	Exchange time	2023-07-31 11:51:28
Order type	LIMIT	Placed by	FA2989
Product	MIS		
Validity	DAY		

View trades   View history   Close

2. External or extra loss: The loss that happened is our fault. We can say that we have control over it. There are some points which we lose.

- Entry into trade without setup.

- FOMO Entry.

- Stop loss set wrong.

- To remain in the trade even after being proven wrong.

- Exiting the trade due to fear. Without any reason.

If there is a loss due to any of these reasons, then the loss is an extra loss which we have control over, that is, we can reduce this type of loss. Since internal loss is not under our control, we cannot do anything about it.

CONFIDENCE

In the world of trading, confidence is not such a thing that if you hold on to it, the work will be done. Confidence is not that I will make money from the market today, confidence is that after six consecutive losses you are ready for the seventh trade with the same mindset and the same strategy. No strategy works 100% in the market.

When the trade is going well and targets are being achieved then our confidence also remains good. But when the stop loss is hit then our confidence also falls. And if more than three stop losses come in a single turn, then the confidence falls drastically and it becomes difficult to maintain the rules. And once even one rule is broken, the scope for error increases. In such a situation, it is difficult to maintain confidence, but in the world of trading you can trust only one person and he is on the move.

IGNORING STOP LOSS

Look, although I talked about stop loss in the strategy rules, I talked about it only about the strategy, but now I am talking about it because many people avoid stop loss. Take a trade but do not place a stop loss thinking that I am sitting in front of the screen, as soon as the trade moves in my Favor I sit and as soon as it moves against me, I will exit. So let me tell you that this can be the biggest mistake of all. Because when trading positions start going into loss then you become emotional, then we do not even realize the seriousness of what is going on in the real world, then we start doing such things which we have known for years that if a What can happen if you break the rules? But still, we do not pay attention to it. I ask a question, are you a girl? If not, then why are you avoiding stop loss? Although this is a joke, but work should be done only by setting stop loss because stop loss is always useful in saving trading capital.

4. SYSTEM

I am sure you have strategies to achieve success in trading. Your strategy is decided, but is that strategy, right? Even if the strategy is good, there may be some complications, because you know today, the information and data you have today. Prepare a strategy based on that. Strategy is not based on any unknown or unknowable element, rather your strategy means that you think more about today than tomorrow. You should have a set target, should your target be 10x or 100x?

It is important to decide what level you want to reach and how to get there, so that you can keep your work on track. It is important to understand how your strategy is being formed based on the knowledge you have. Your strategy takes your today forward and envisions tomorrow. That is, in many ways, those things and possibilities which may not exist in your experience, but may exist in reality. Or put it this way, what you haven't seen yet, you have to imagine with today's knowledge."

Overall, I want to say that while making a strategy, all kinds of possibilities will have to be considered. No information can be denied. Another thing to keep in mind is whether this strategy will still work in future? If any change is required, will it be easy to make changes? Will we be able to maintain the trading edge even after making changes? Well, strategy is made after thinking deeply on many questions.

FIRST OF ALL, WHY IS THE SETUP AND SYSTEM IMPORTANT?

There is movement in the market. So, he will give the move, it does not mean that we have to take all the moves. We can only take a few moves. Cannot capture all moves. We just have to capture one move well and only then we will become traders. Look, traders can work in many ways, some have setup, some have smart money concept, some have price action, some have computerization, some have trend taking. What's your setup? Are you working with one setup today and another setup the next day? Are you moving from one system to another? If you are doing this then maybe you will make money today but what about tomorrow? What will you do next month, next year? So, it is necessary to have some system for that. Setup is necessary. On which you can work well.

My aim was not just to tell you this strategy. Rather, how to make a strategy together, how to make a trading setup, a trading system? Had to tell this also. Because this same strategy does not suit everyone. Everyone's style is different. Everyone's method of working, timing, age, win-rate, risk to reward, all this is different. In this way, even if you copy an entire system or strategy, there is no benefit. The reason is that it does not suit everyone to trade with the same style. But if the other person's strategy as well as his trading style suits you, then you can do it. If anyone wants to copy. By copying I mean that both his trading strategy and trading style will have to be copied completely. If you can do this then only you should copy it. If not, then you should make your own strategy which suits you.

Now many people here will ask how a strategy can be made like this. So for those people I would like to say that it is okay, if you cannot create any new strategy or setup or system then there are many big trades in this world, look at their strategies. It is possible that the same strategy may not suit your trading style, but you can create a new system similar to it by changing many rules and regulations. I also did not create this strategy myself. When a friend told me, I did back testing, made changes in many rules and regulations, this strategy was created after a lot of modification. Because if the implementation of the strategy becomes different, then the strategy becomes different from what inspired it. There is no harm in that.

What is the system after all? Trading system means a complete strategy in which all the decisions are decided in advance. This means that when you take a trade, you do not need to think about anything separately, because everything is already decided. You just have to follow the strategy and its rules. If you understand in other words.

Actually, the system is where trading has to be done only after deciding everything in advance. By everything here, I mean the entry point of the trade, exit point, stop loss, everything. It is not that any particular pattern has formed in the market. If I find a particular support, a particular area or any strategy, I will take the trade. All my things are already decided. It is not the case that today I am trading with some strategy, tomorrow I am trading with some other strategy and on the next day I am trading with something else, I am taking trades after seeing any new strategy. Doesn't happen like this. There is a particular strategy. In which everything from the entry to the exit of the trade is already decided. This is because when the trade is going on, no other thought comes to my mind and I execute my trade peacefully.

A SYSTEM TELLS YOU WHAT TO DO WHEN

Because everything is included in the system. When to do what? Every single thing, from entry price to stop loss, even the target, everything is decided in advance. It is as if when the trade is going on we do not have any second thought as to what to do next? Because everything is decided according to the rules. And that's why emotions are completely out of the question while trading.

WAITING FOR TRADE ENTRY

The most difficult task in this is waiting, which not everyone is able to do. Having a system saves them from these things. Random Trading, Revenge Trading, Over Trading, Early Exit, Late Exit.

TRADE MANAGEMENT

Trade management in which entry point, stop loss point, exit point, RRR, position size all should be known before taking the trade. The rules of this strategy have been made like this. By following which, complete trade management can be done.

You have to make money with right approach

What does it mean? What I want to say about making money through the right approach is to assume that you took some action and made money from it. By action I mean that for some reason a trade was taken which was worth a penny. Give him a guess or any word and the trade works and you make money. And then the second time you take the trade for the same reason and make a loss, then you will feel that you did something wrong whereas the reason was the cost due to which you made money in the first trade. Sometimes you might have heard that it made good money, big money in one go, which was made for some reason, the same thing happened again and again but now it is not making the same money, the reason behind it is the same right approach. Don't know or don't understand how to make money in the right way. That's why I say that "if you make money with wrong way then you don't understand right way"

TRADING IN A HURRY

I have seen and it has happened to me many times that we take trades in a hurry. Trading in a hurry. First of all, let me ask you this question, have you seen any big trader working or taking decisions in a hurry? No, I am saying that if you are taking trades in a hurry, then you are doing it wrongly. Are you trading? A trader works very calmly, he knows that entry is going to come in his trade, where the entry will be made, he prepares how many positions to take and as soon as he gets the entry, he enters very fast, and manages the trade in a very professional manner.

Now let us talk about some questions which remain in the mind of new traders.

1. **Should we talk to our trader and non-trader friends about the work we are doing or in other words, whatever strategy we are working on?** So, I would like to tell you that yes, you should definitely talk to your trader friends, that way we will get the answer to how the strategy can work better and how it can be better. Because it is possible that what I know and what my friend knows, by combining both these things can create something new or something that can stop the loss to some extent and yes, one more thing is possible that your And if your friend's opinion is completely different, then let us force ourselves to think a little that how far can I go by doing what you are thinking, oh if I listen to my friend then how far can I go. If you can do the calculation then yes, you should talk to your trader friend about trading but do not talk about it to a non-trader, because he may not understand you, but on the contrary, he may also misguide you. Is. There is another reason why you should not talk to a non-trader about your trading. He will have many reasons for not trading and there will be one or two who can influence you.

2. **Should we tell our relatives about our trading career?** See, here also the same thing applies to traders and non-traders, if your relative is a trader then yes, definitely tell him but if he is a non-trader then it is better not to talk much about it.

3. **How do we know whether the strategy or setup we are making is right or wrong?** And if it is true, can this system be run for lifetime?

Yes, this is a very difficult question, but what I know or my philosophy is this - when you have designed a strategy and back testing it is showing profits, and you have implemented it for a period of time and you have seen that it is also profitable. And that too with consistency, then this strategy is correct. And whether this will remain true in future also or not, the answer is, along with the time zone of the market, changes will have to be made in the strategy as well, some rules will have to be changed. What I am saying is that the strategy needs to be refined over time and if you can do it right then yes, it works.

Some lines written by the author.

"If is a chance to make money then make it otherwise chance is will make you."

"If you make money with wrong way then you don`t understand right way."

"Stock market is a place where a mistake means losing money."

"Hello,

I hope you enjoy my book, "One Stock One Strategy". If you have a moment, I'd appreciate any feedback you could share.

Please email me at pradipnakum78@gmail.com or leave a review on Amazon

I would really appreciate it if you could take a one minutes to write a short review on the Amazon platform, it would be of great help to me.

Thank you, Pradip Nakum"